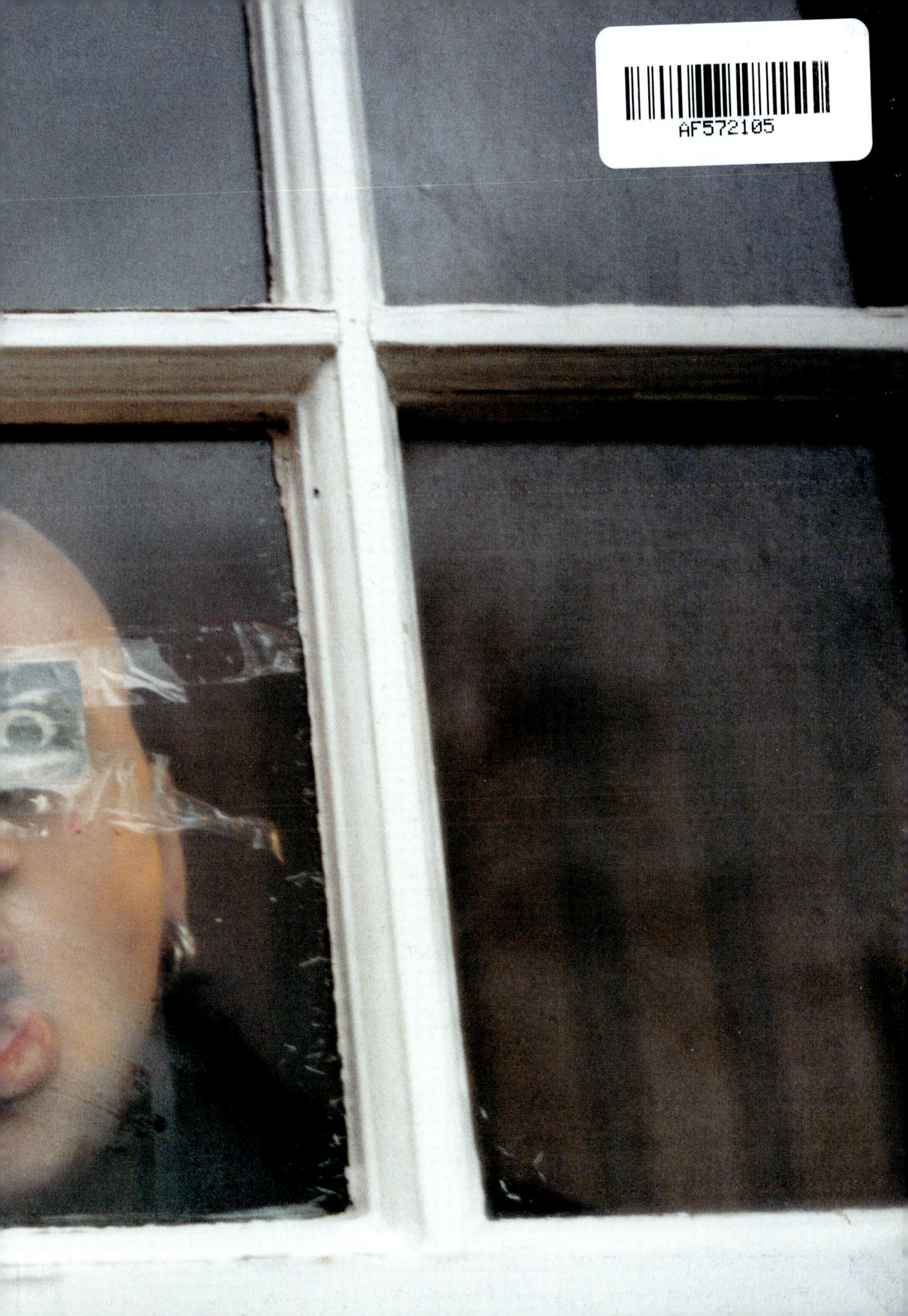

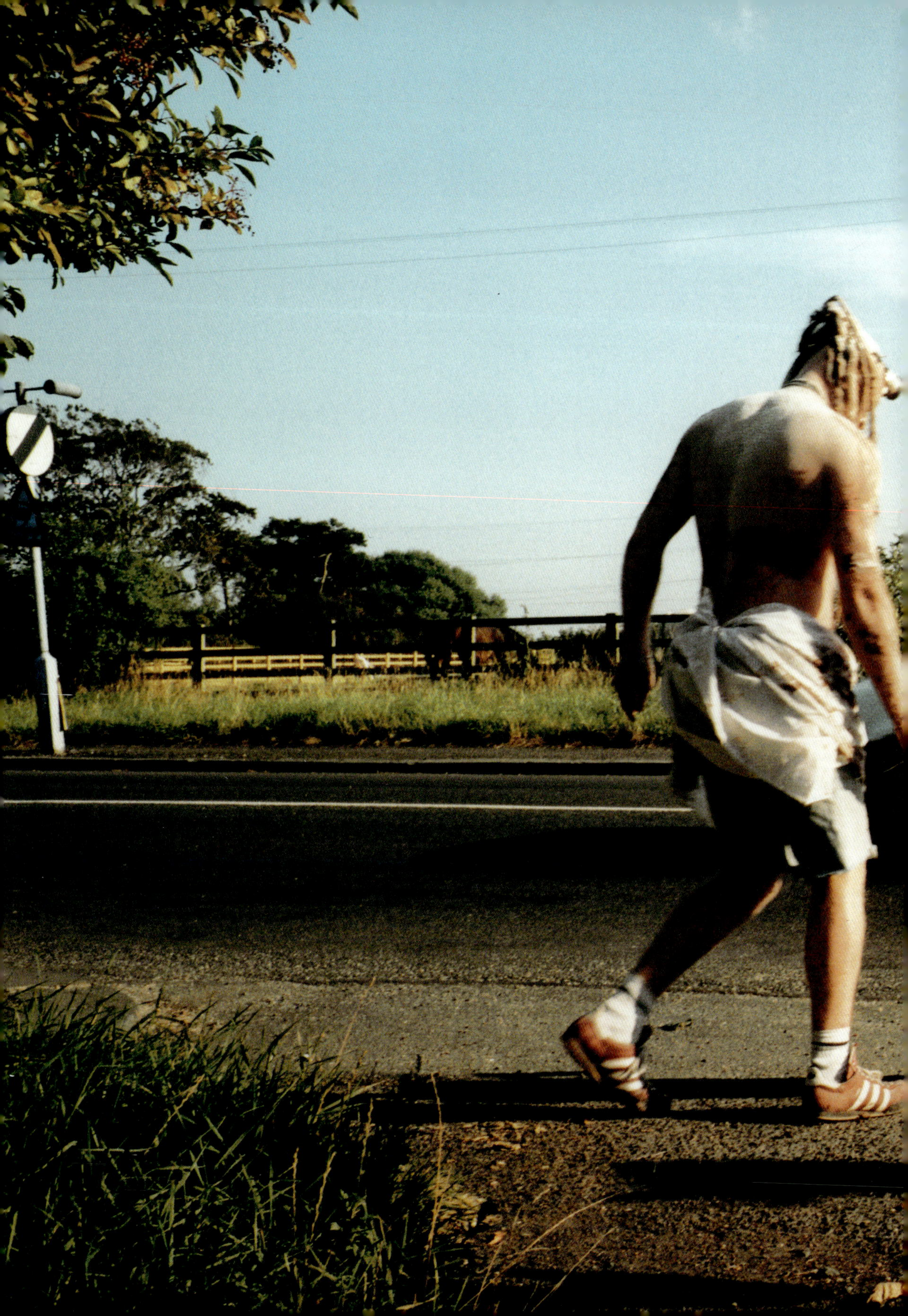

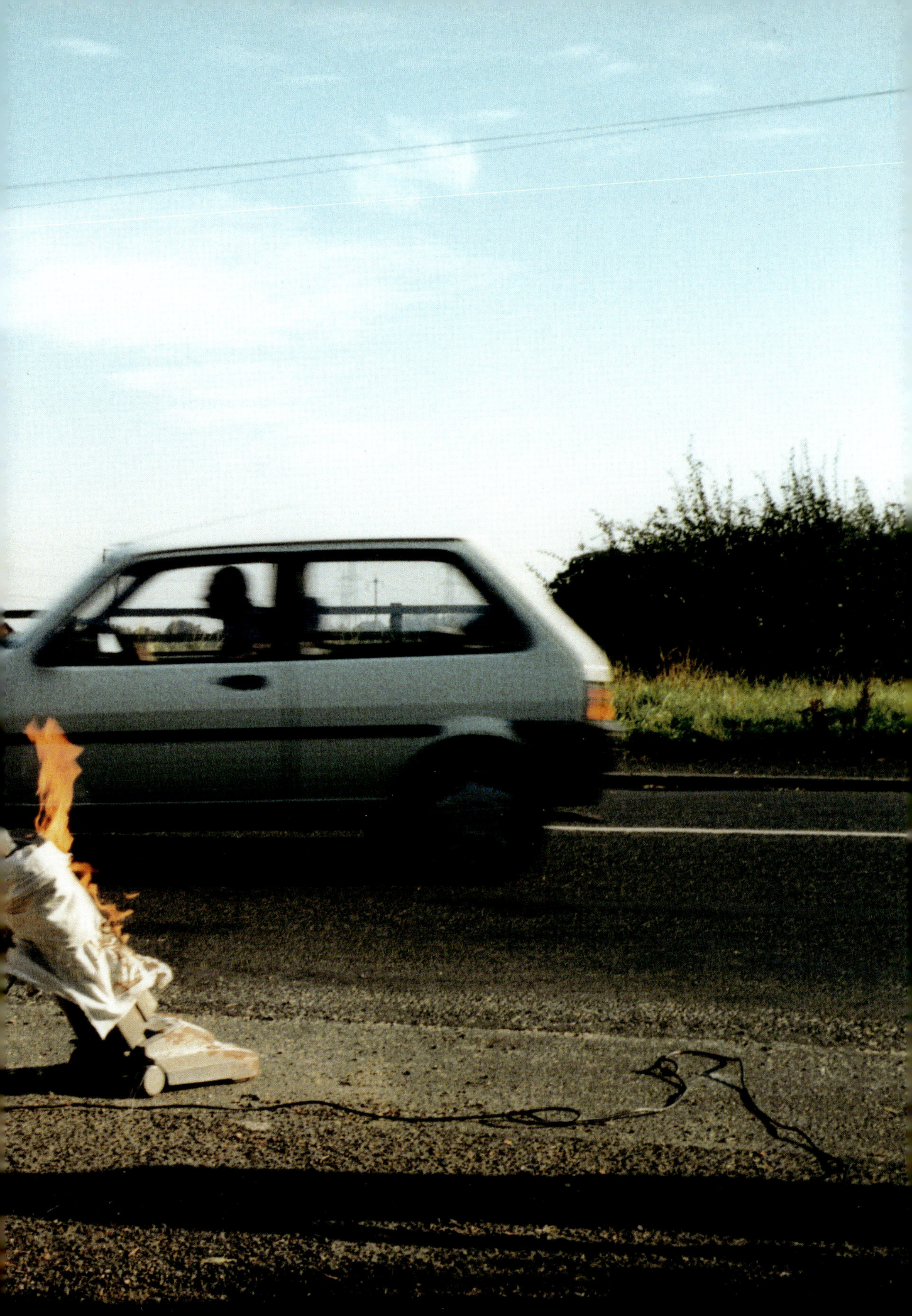

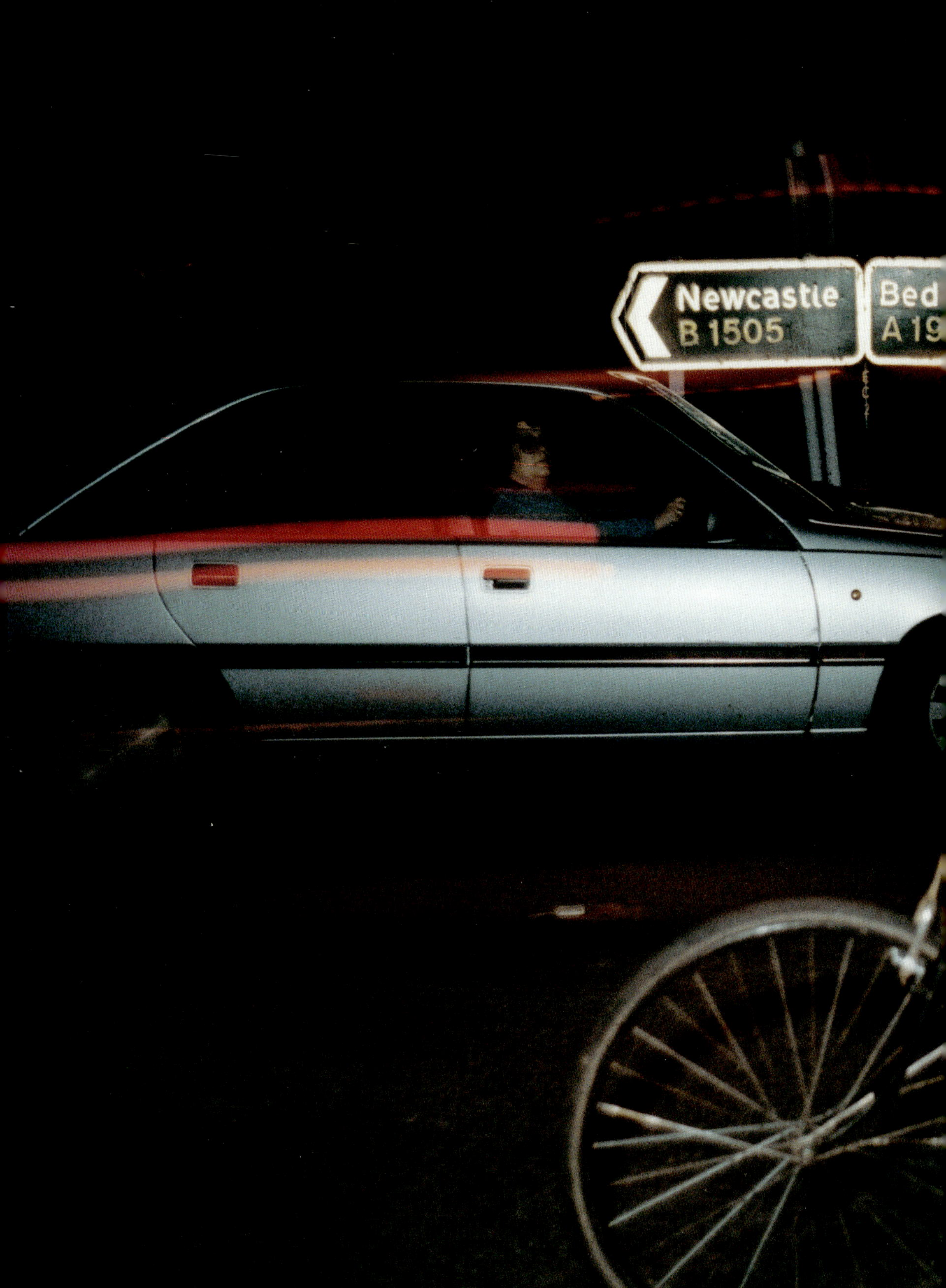
Newcastle
B 1505
Bed
A 19

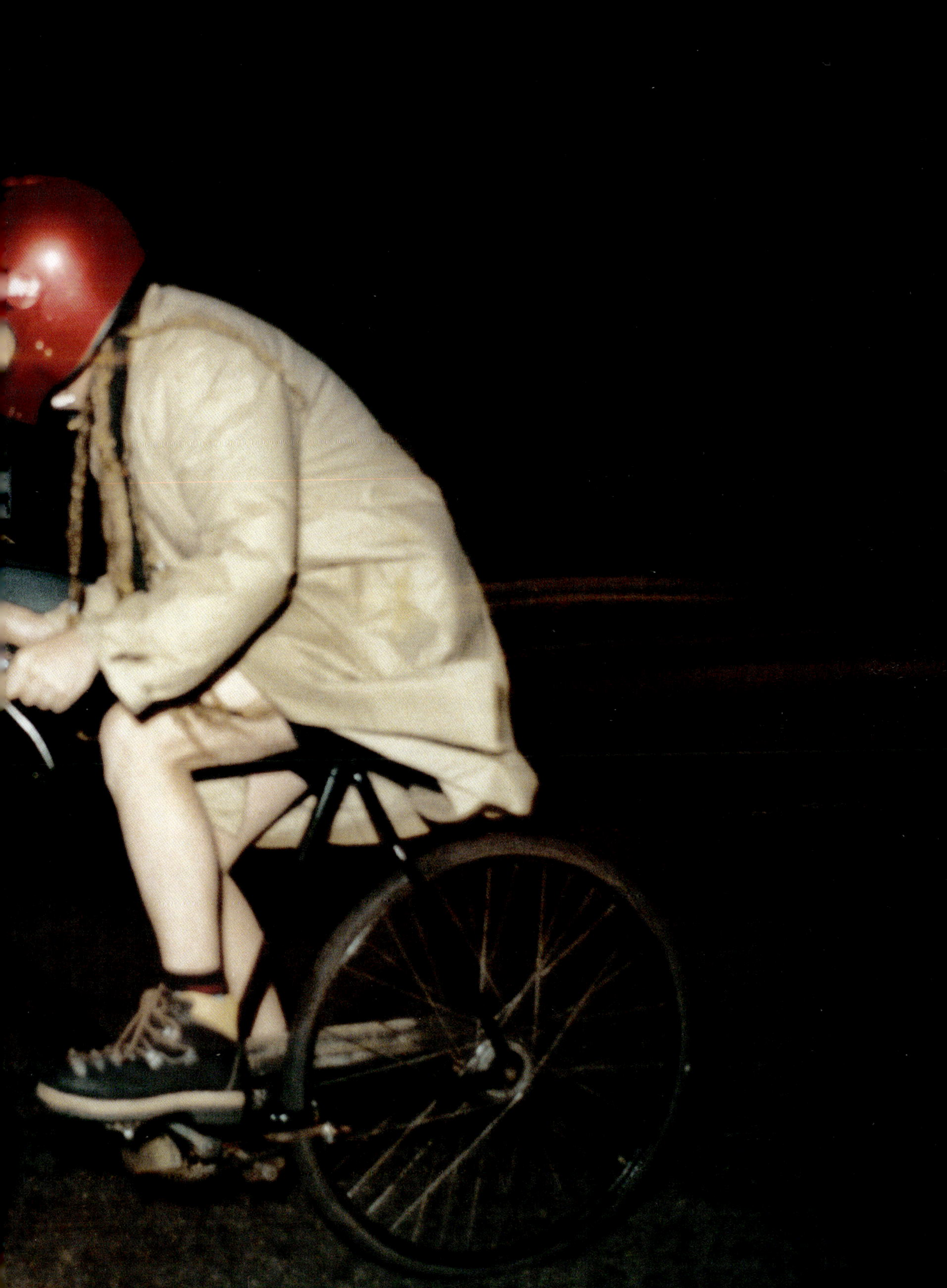

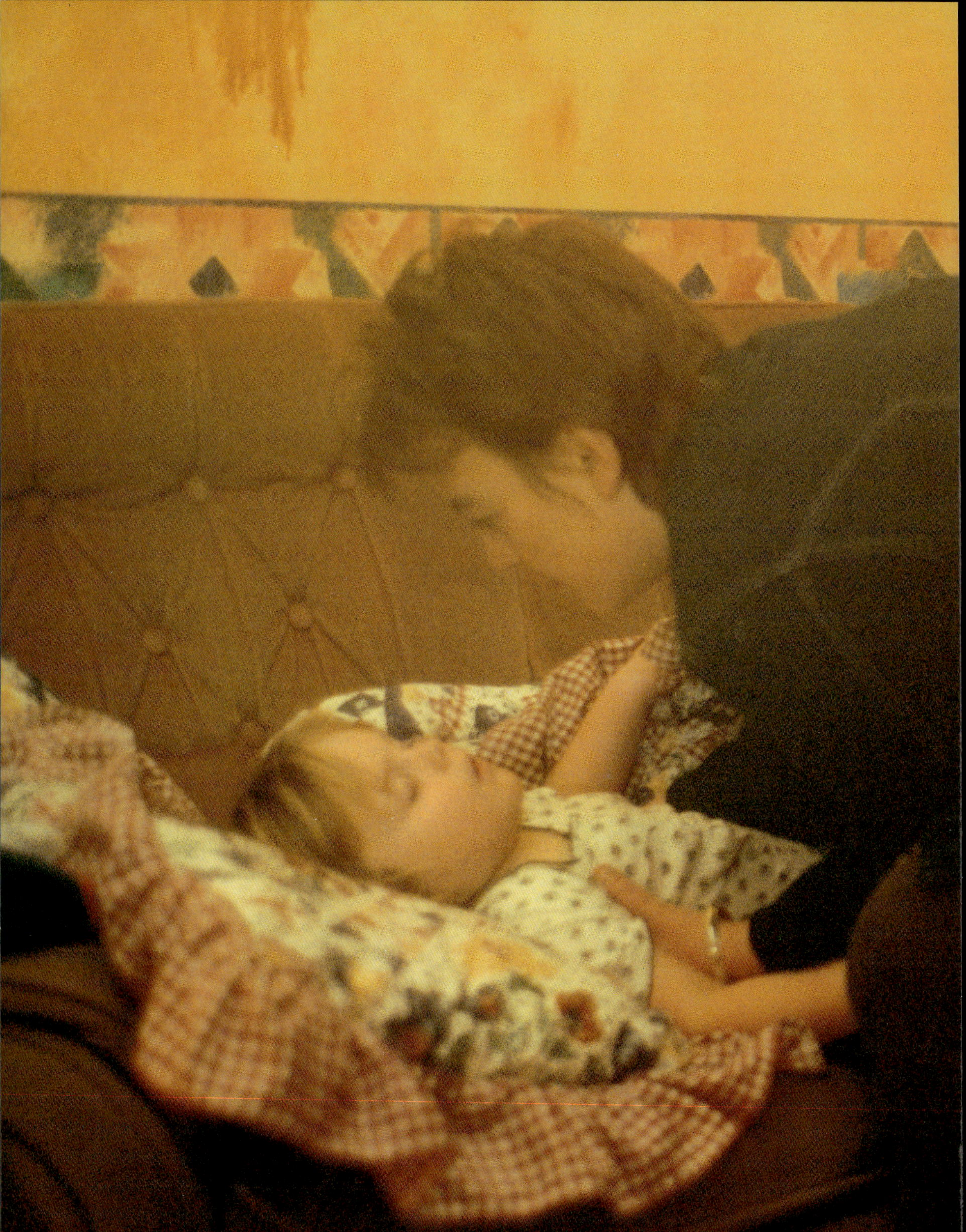

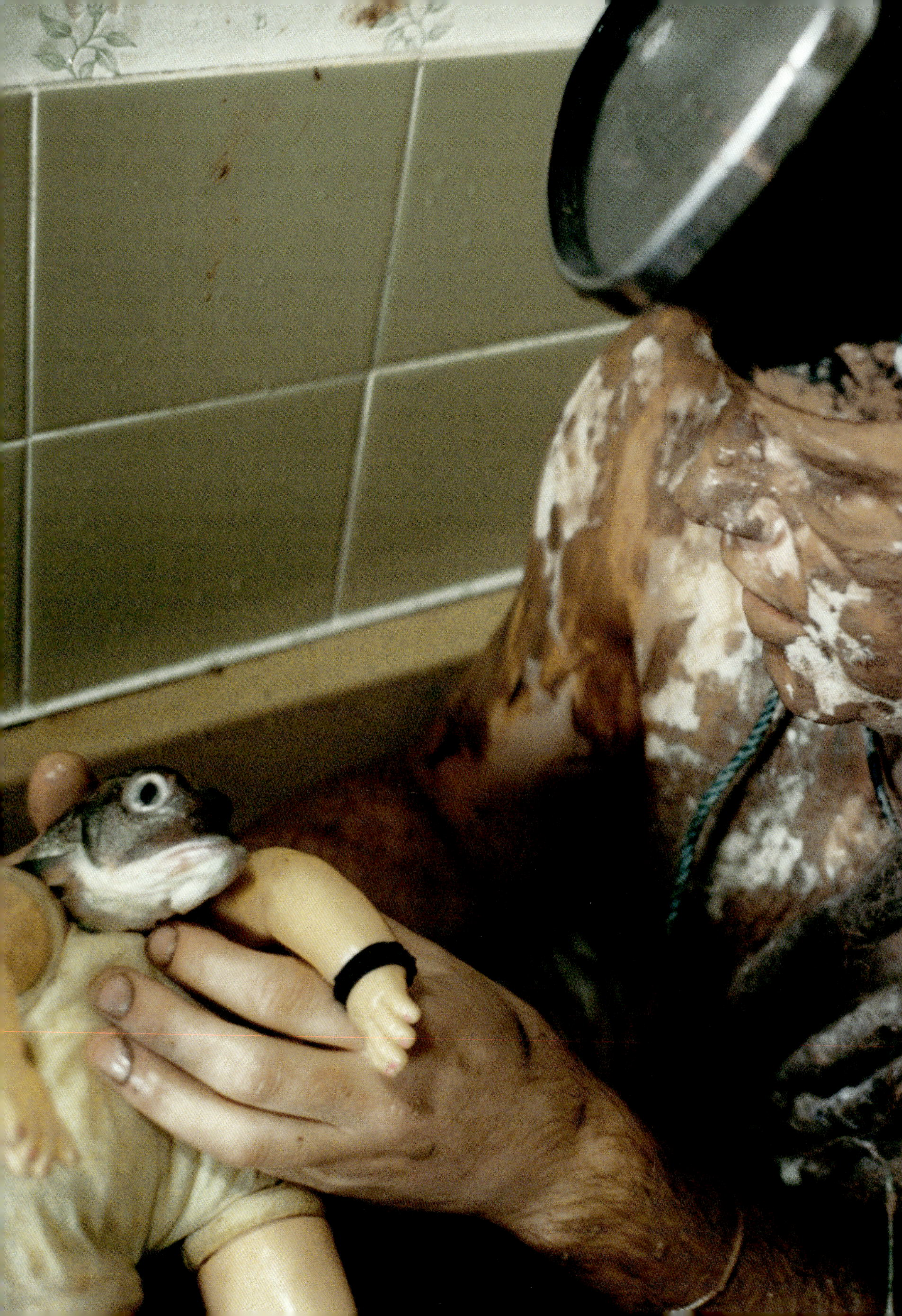

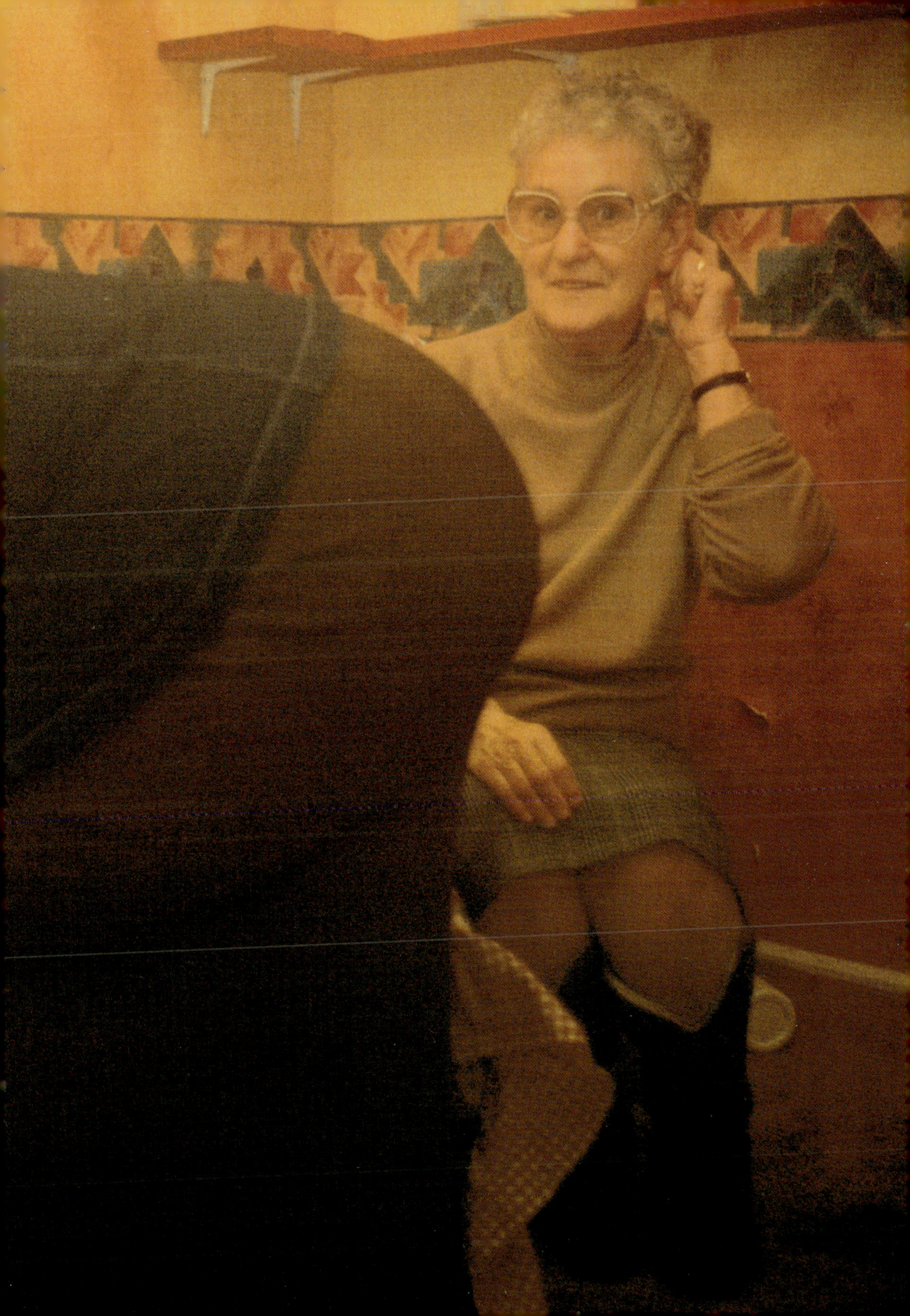

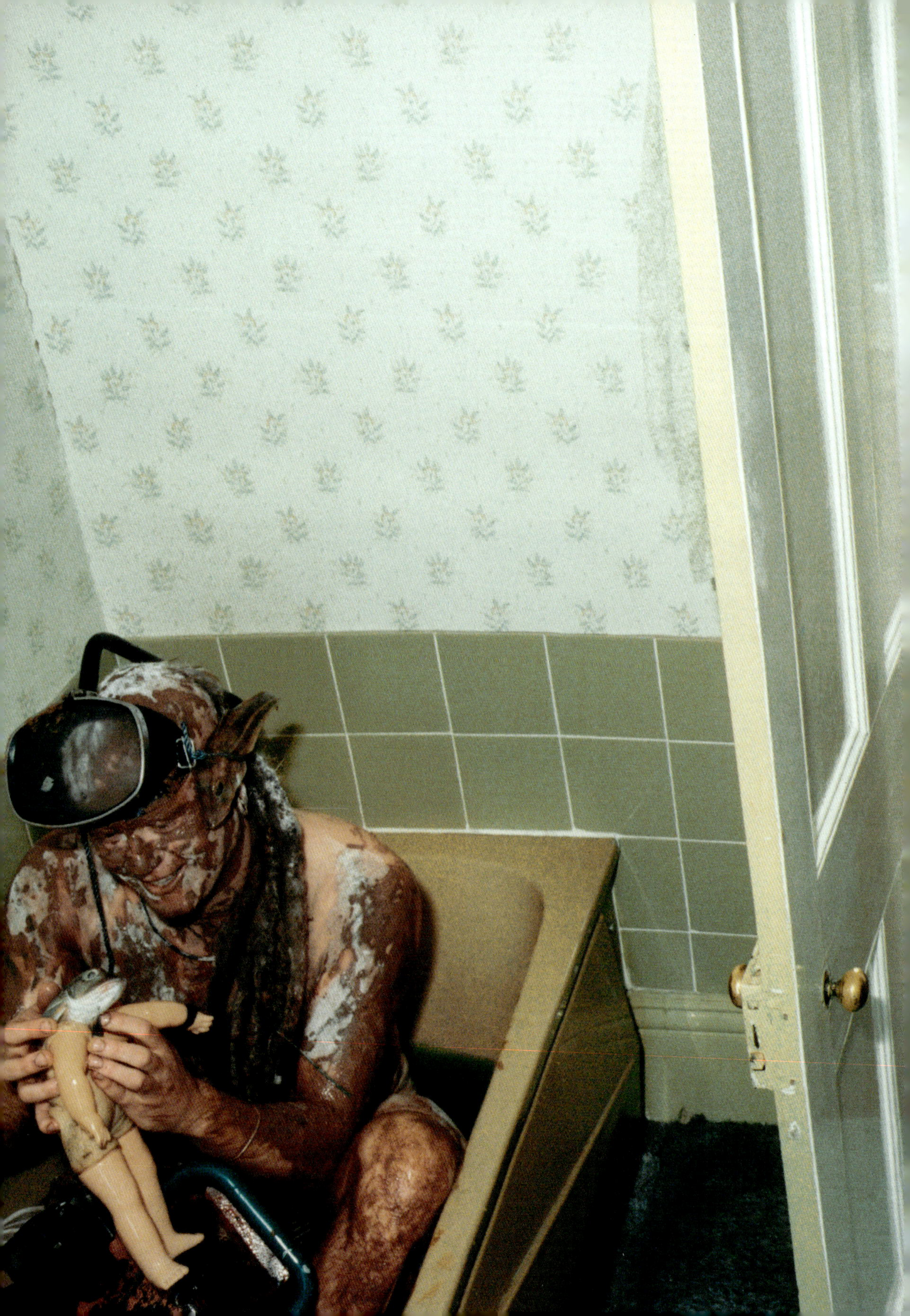

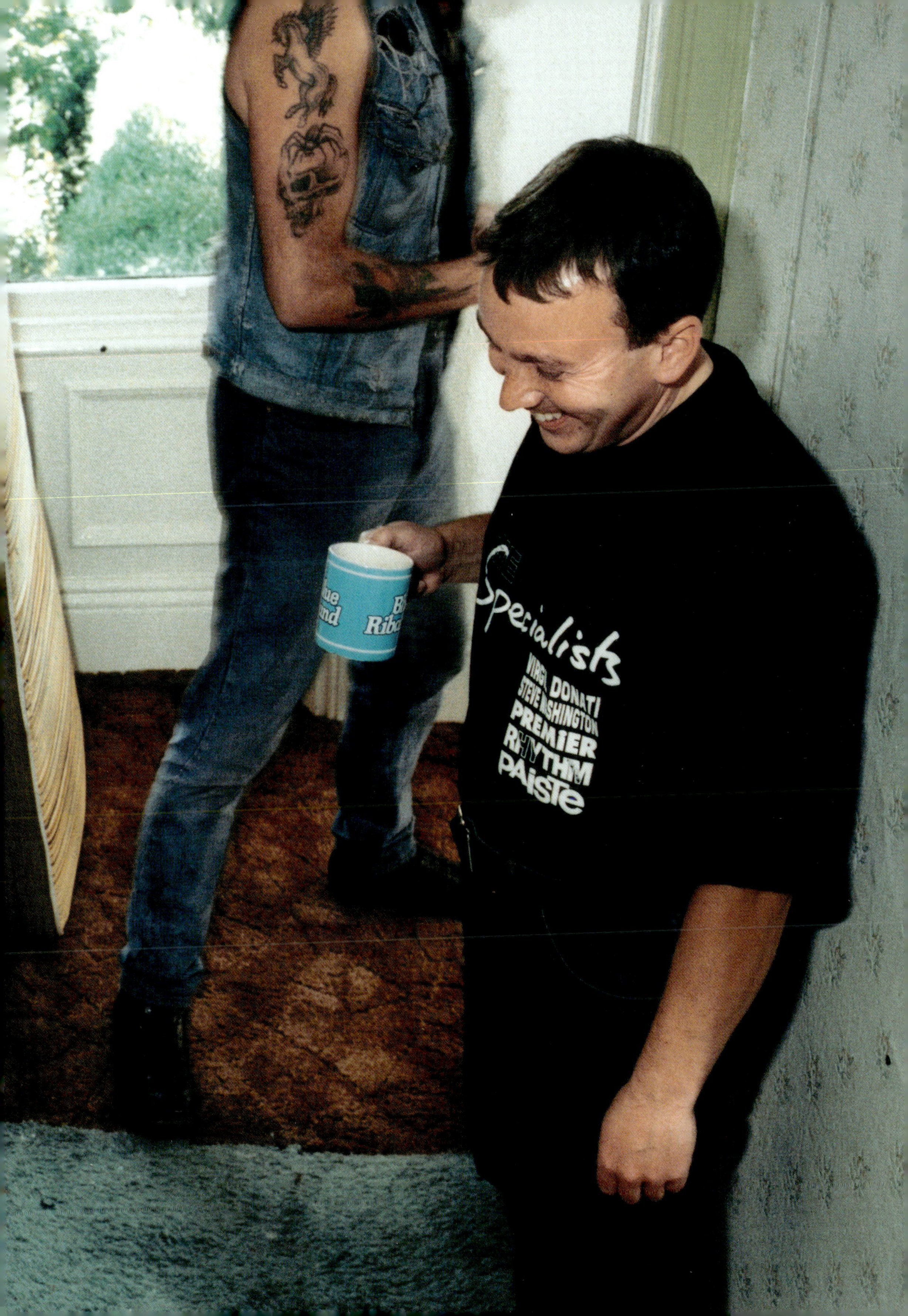
Specialists
PREMIER
RHYTHM
PAISTE

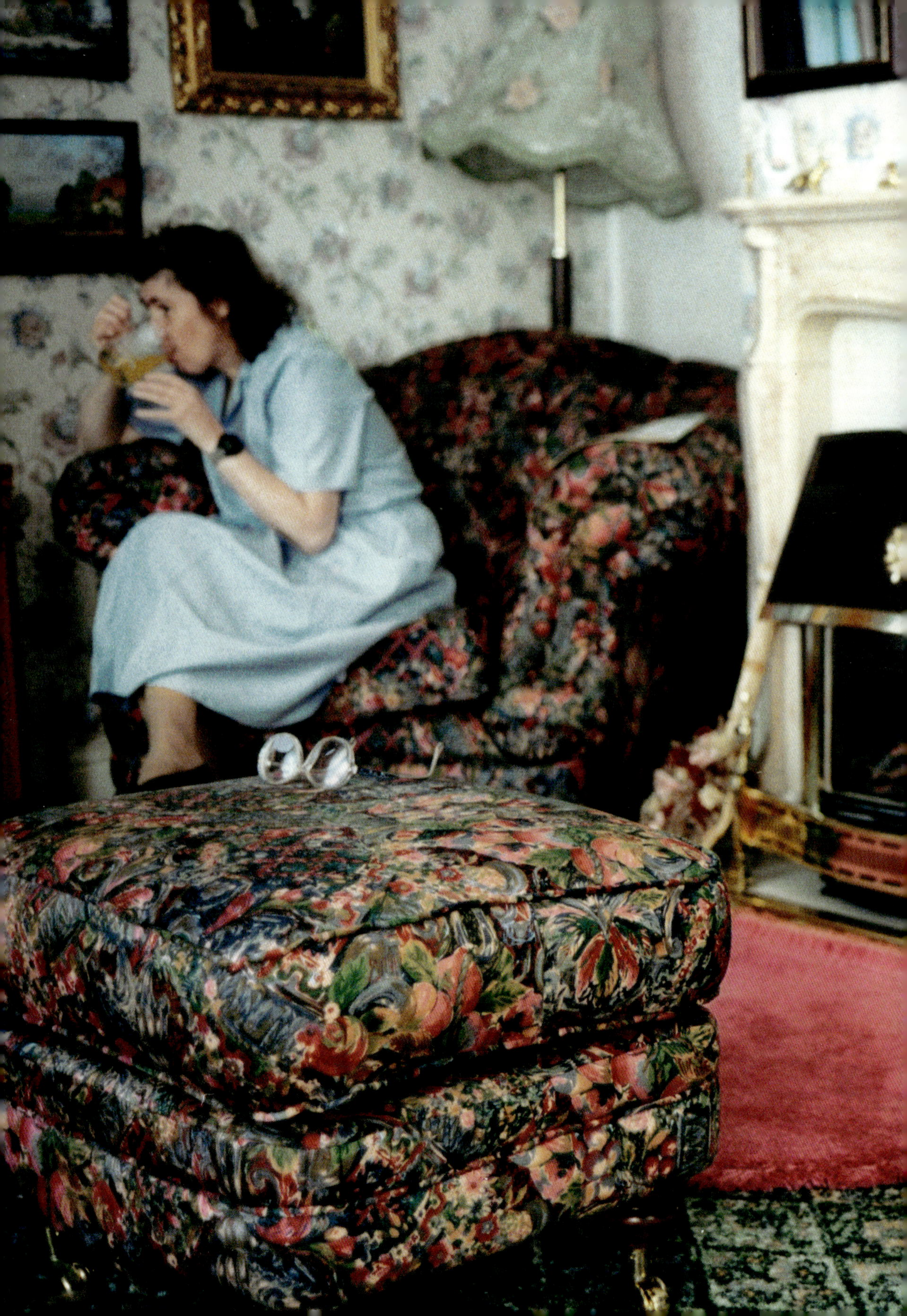

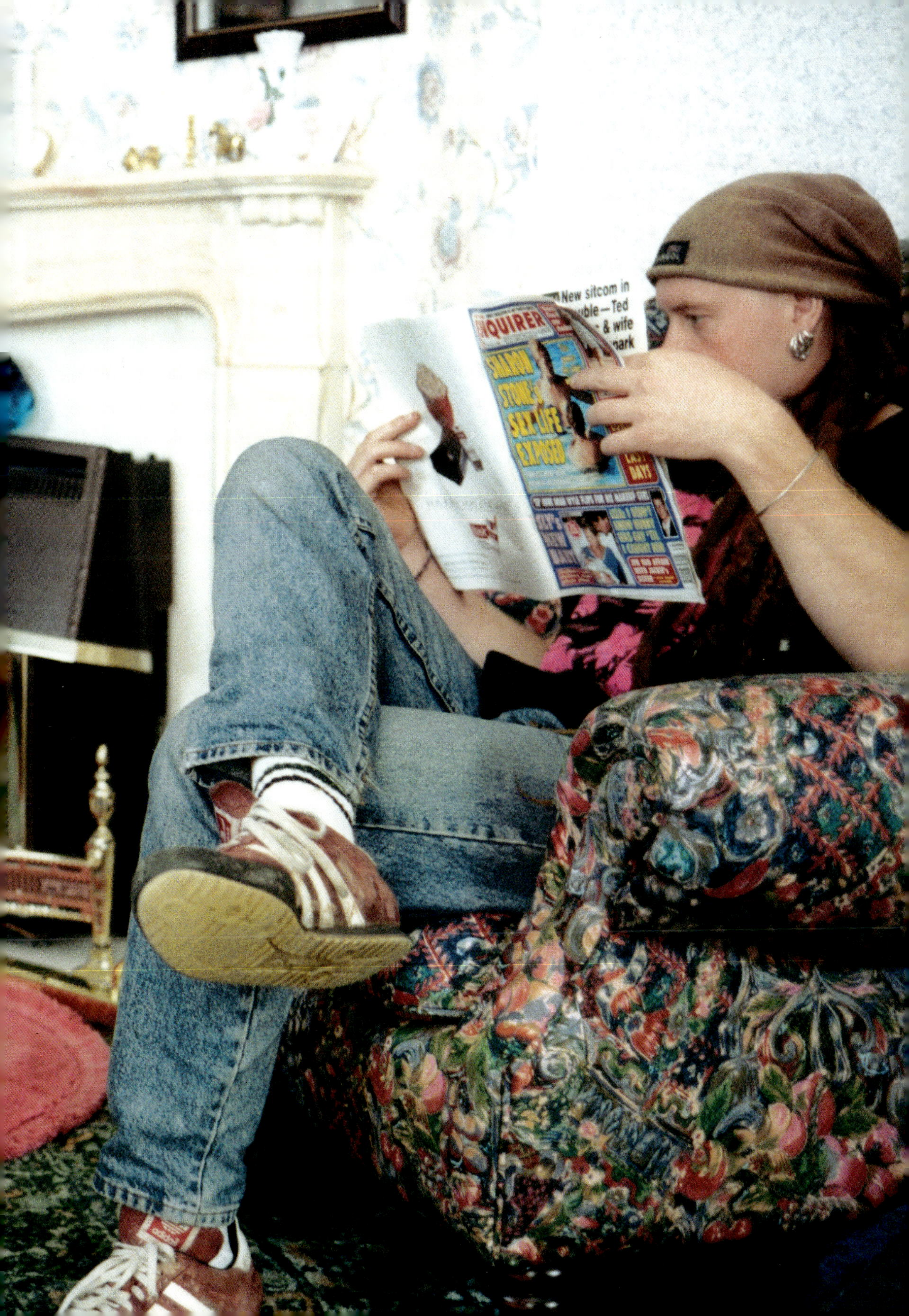
New sitcom in
QUIRER
SHARON STONE'S SEX LIFE EXPOSED
LAST DAYS!

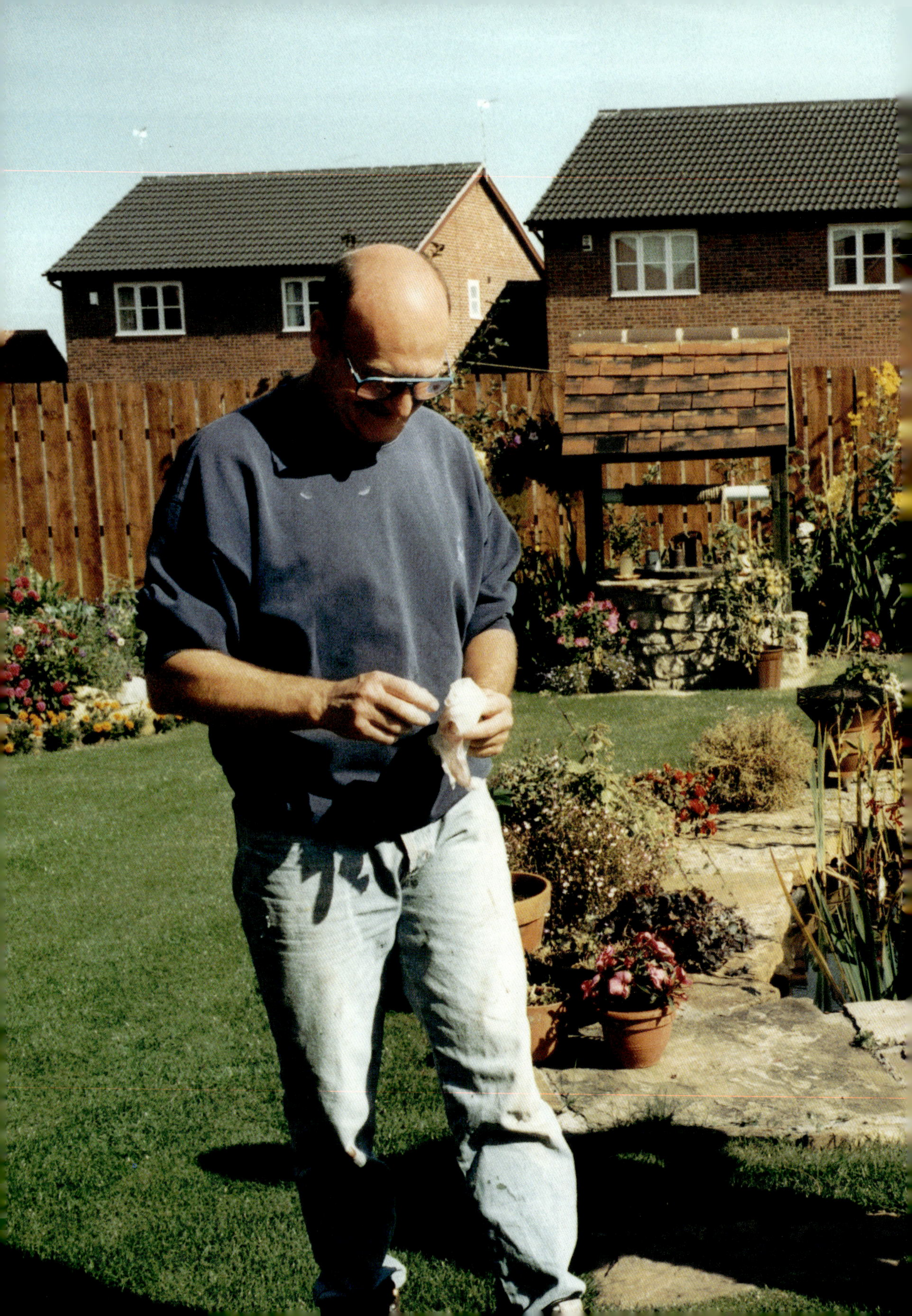

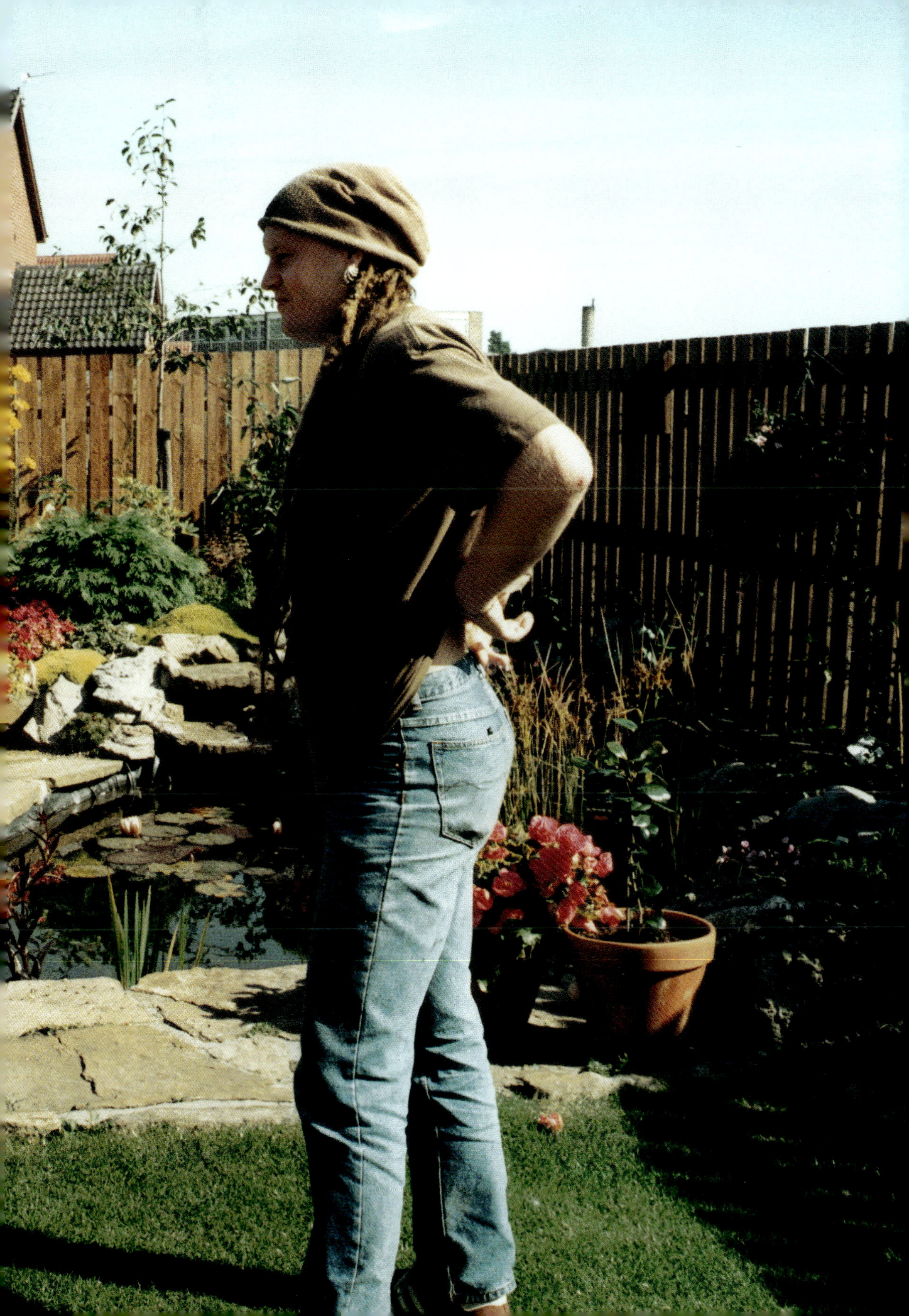

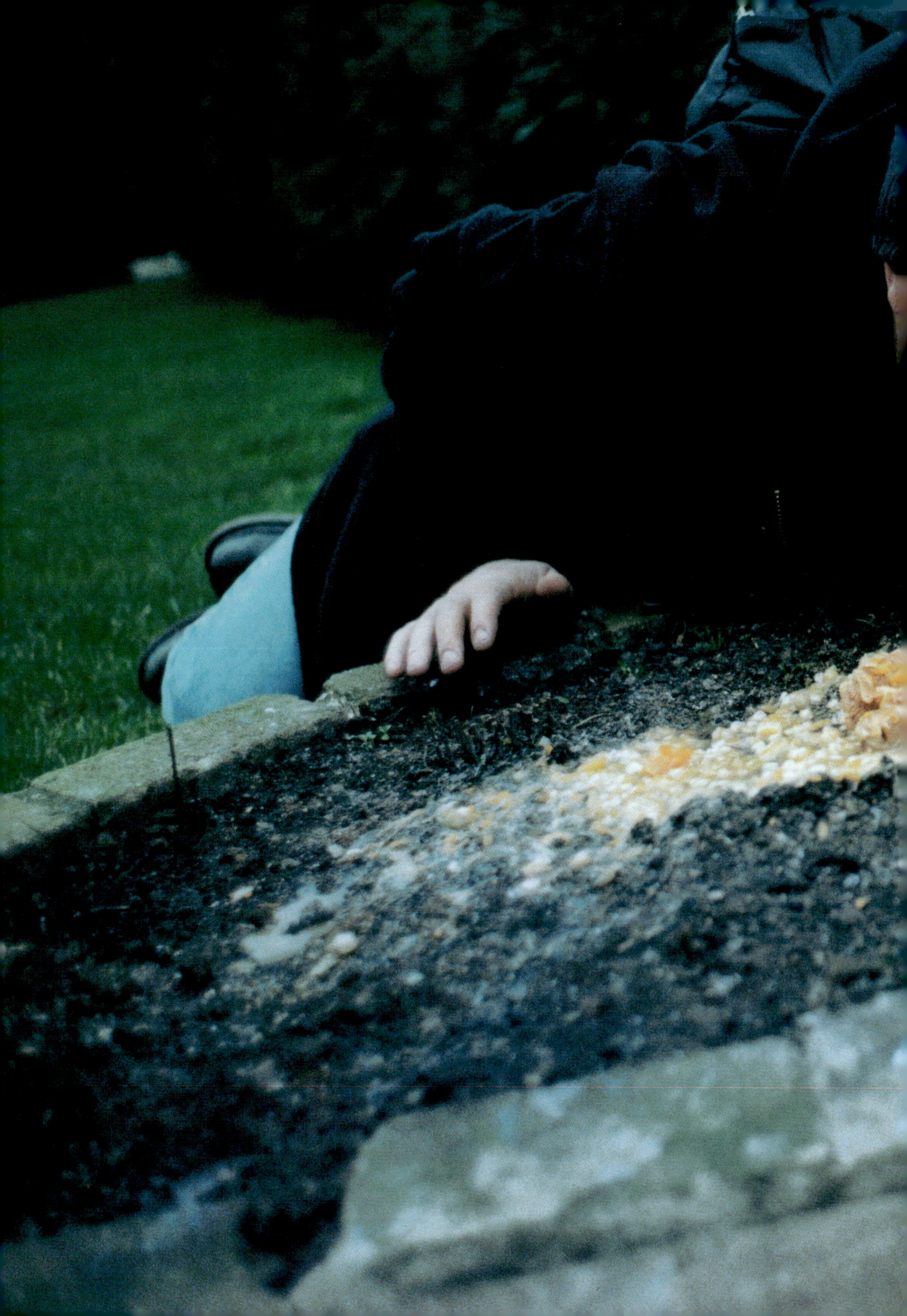

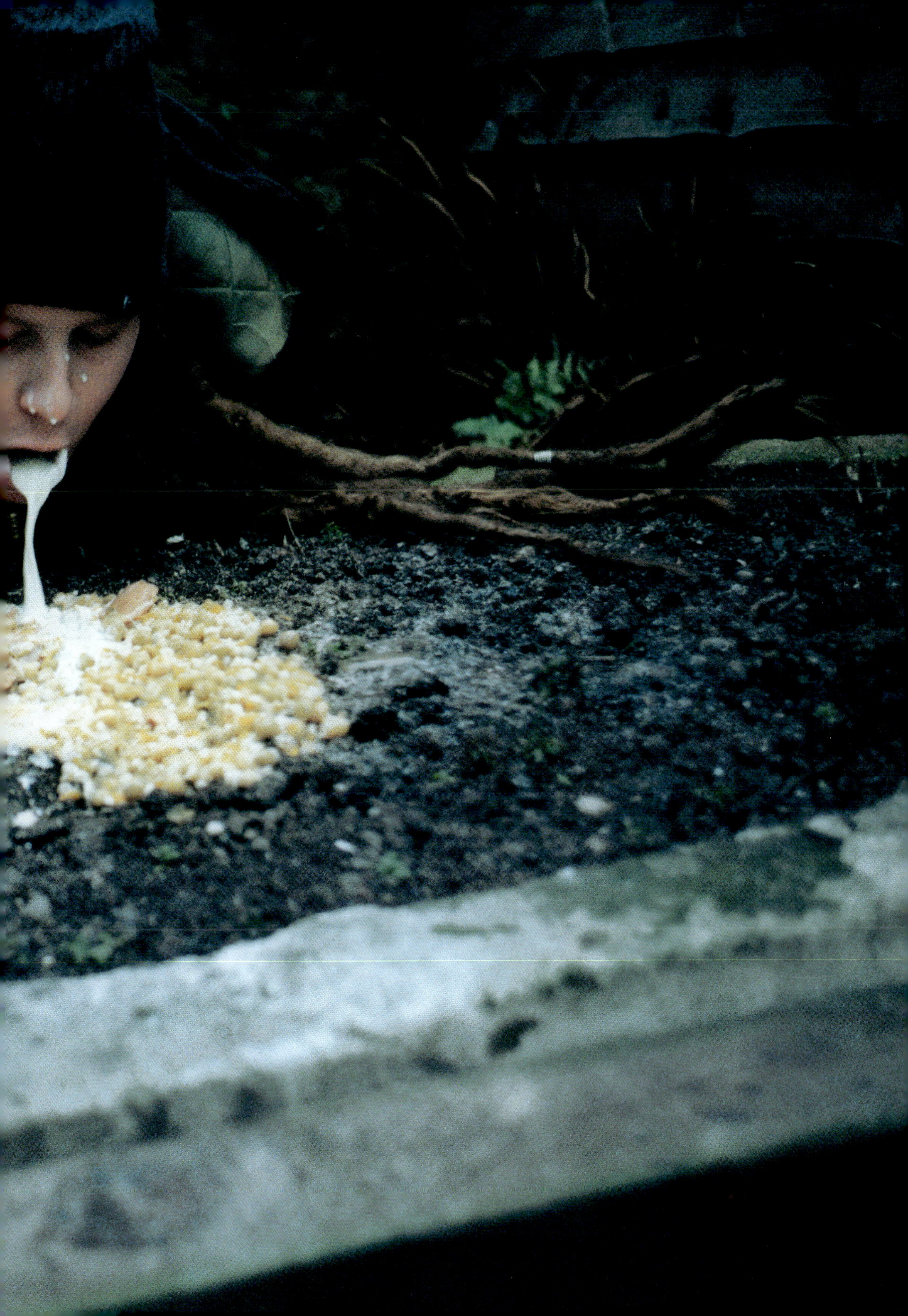

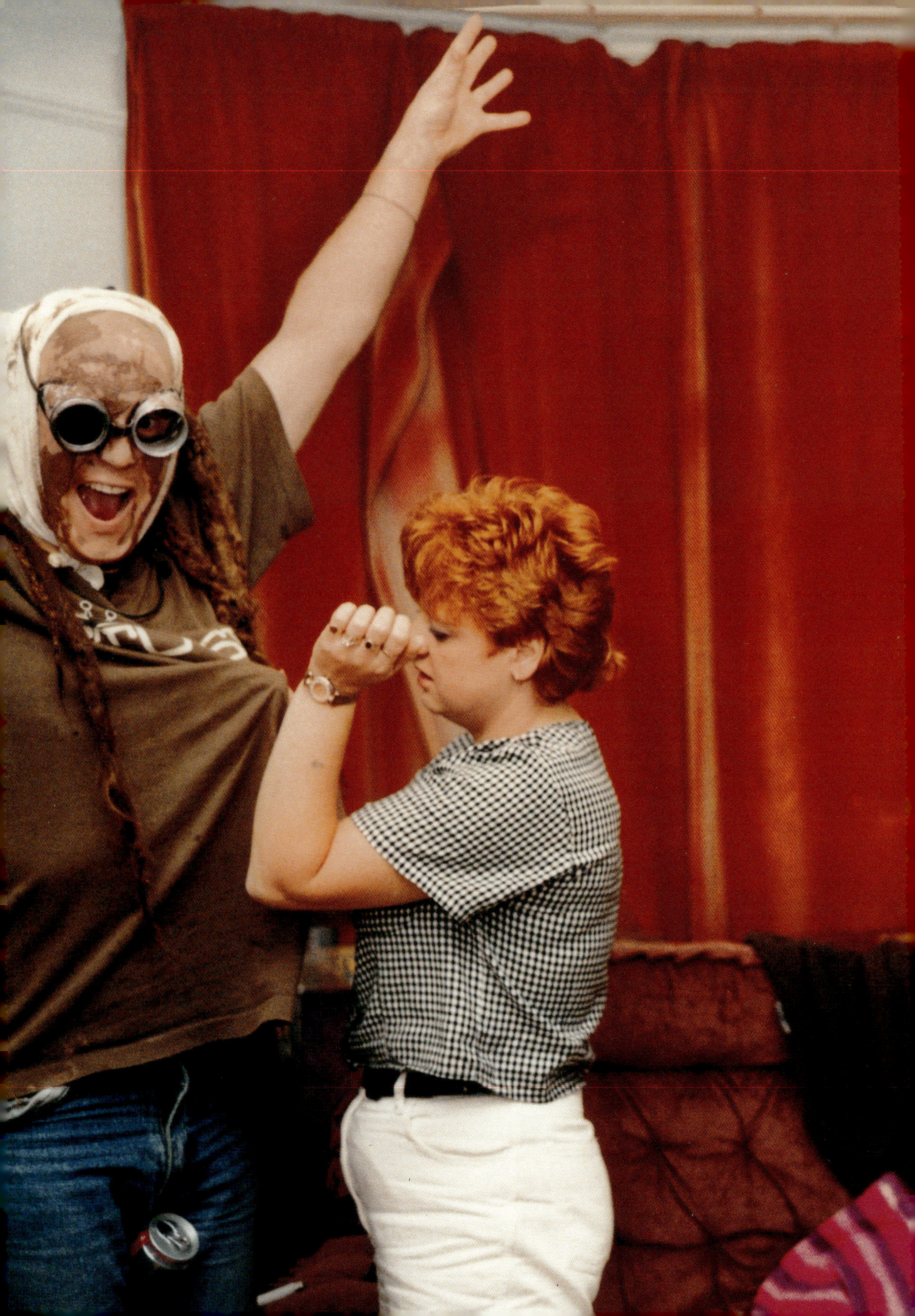

Sad tales of long-running and
Sometimes violent family disputes,
Over money, in-laws, inheritance,
And a cup of tea.

J. Y.

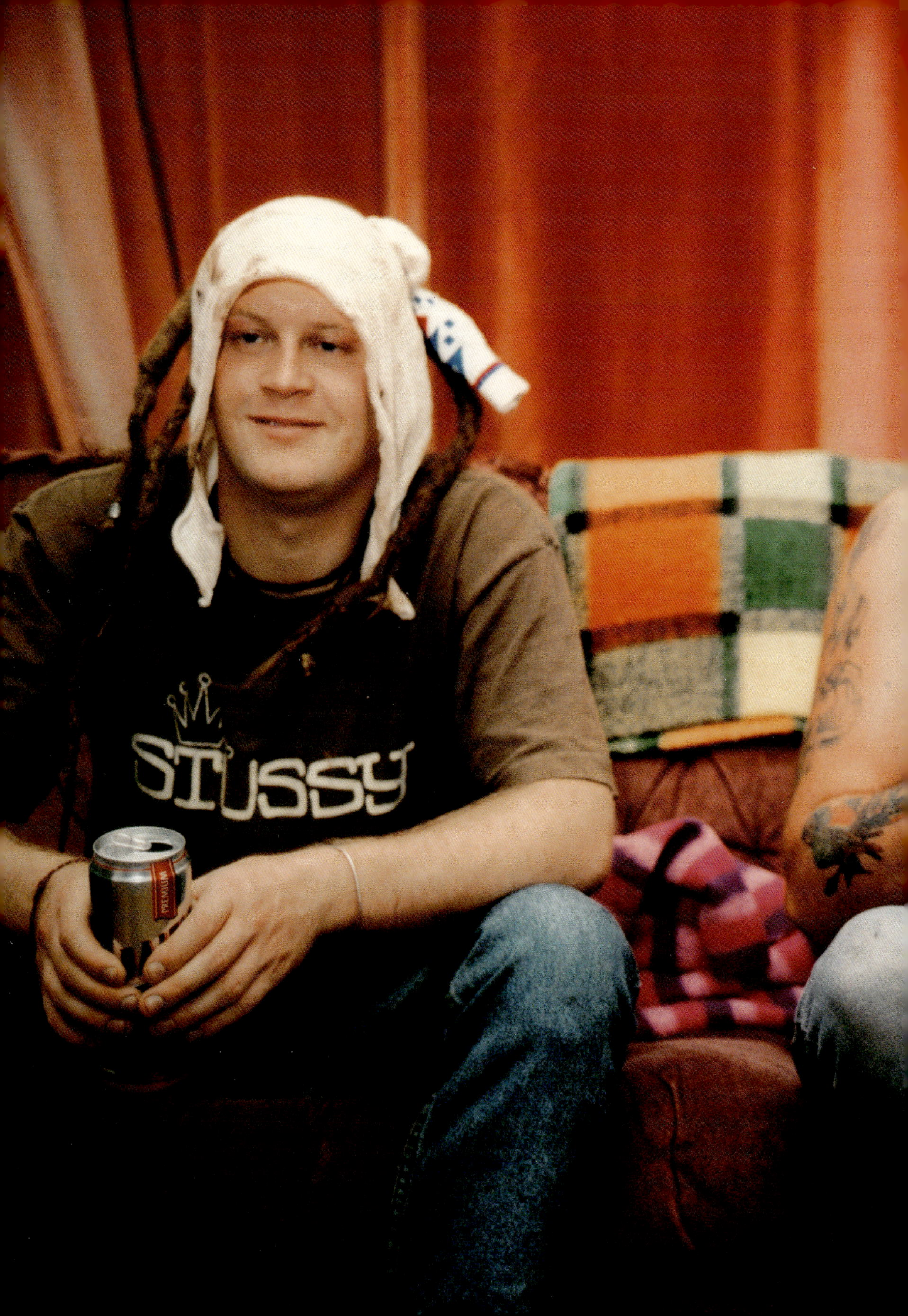
STUSSY

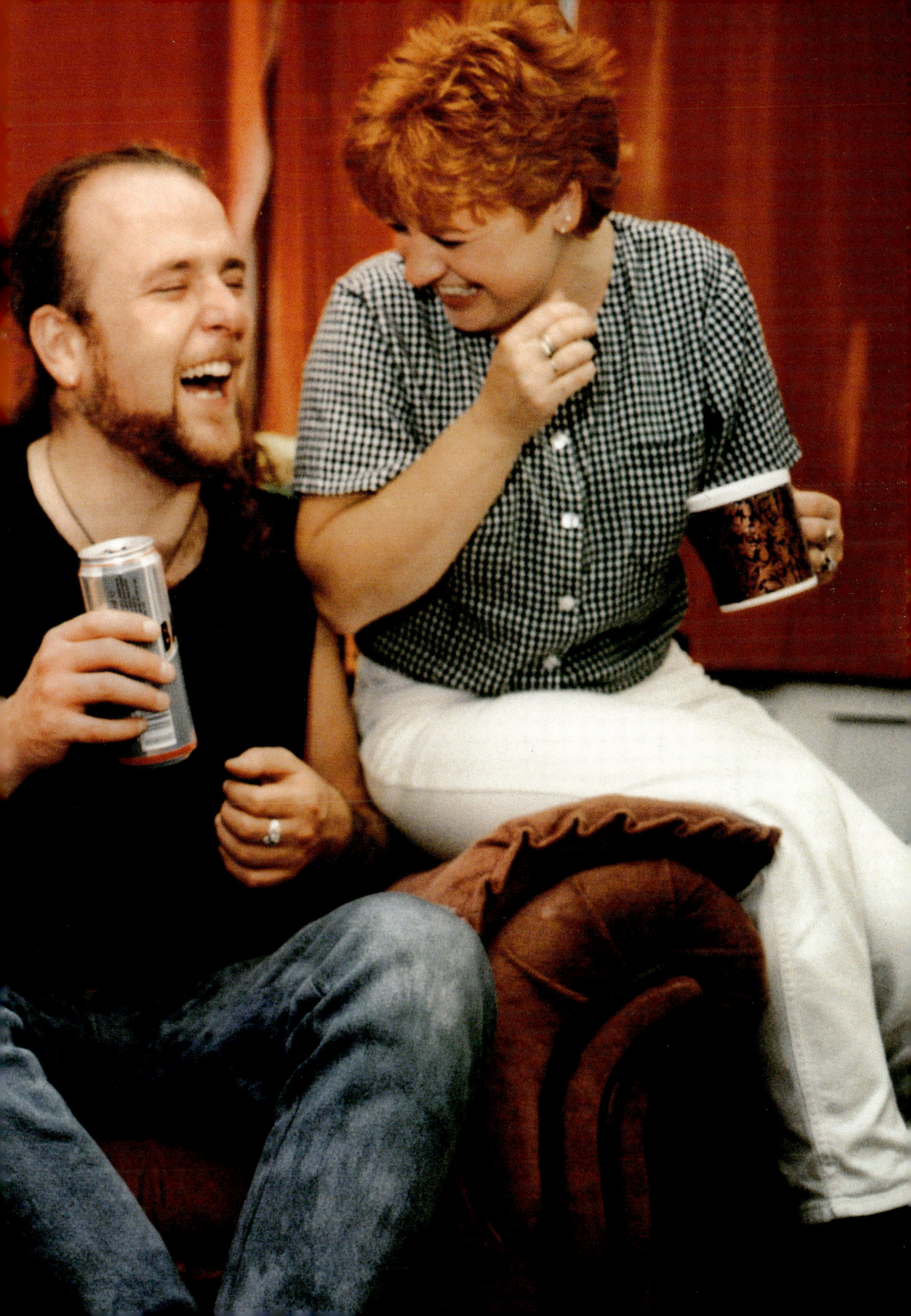

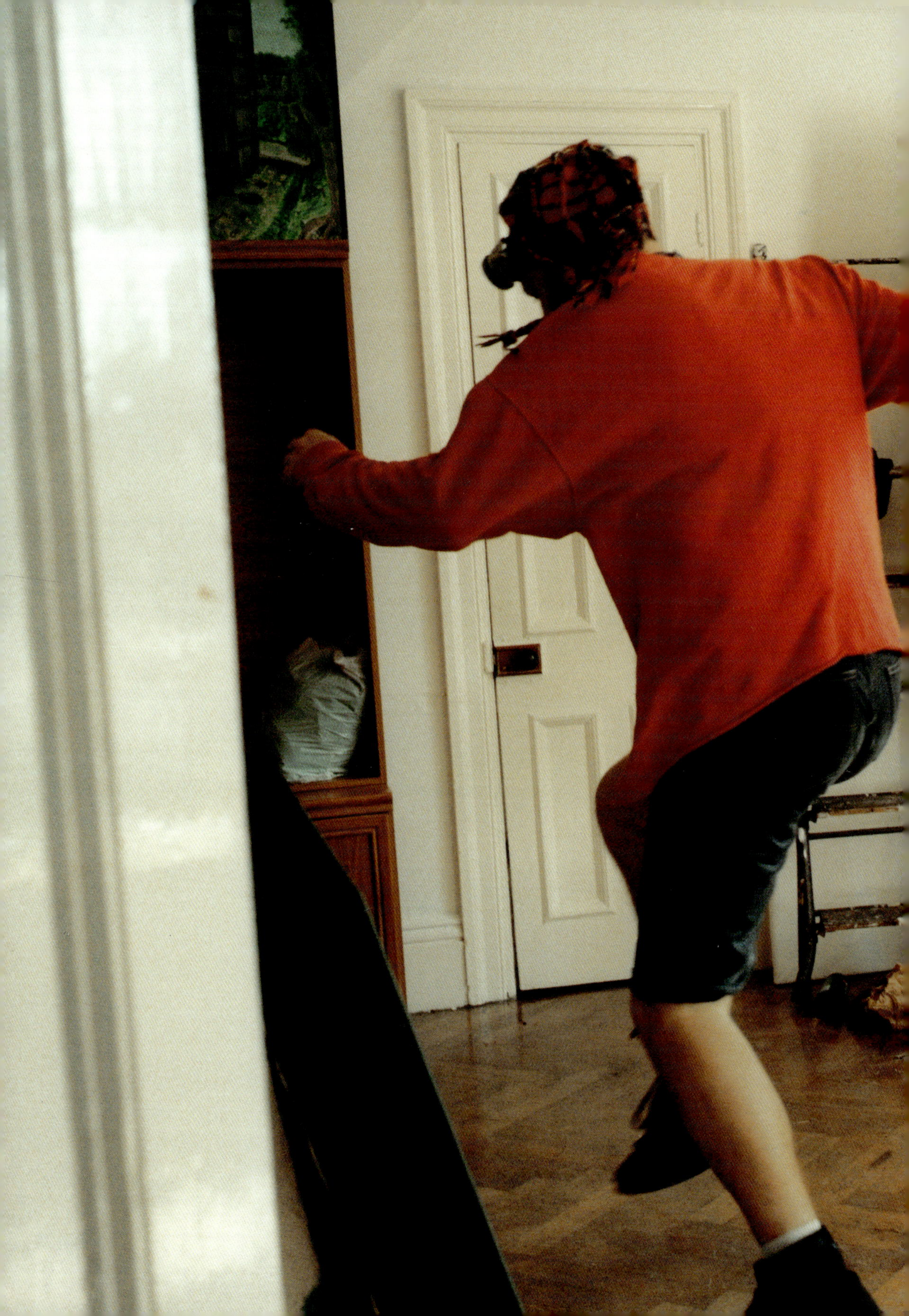

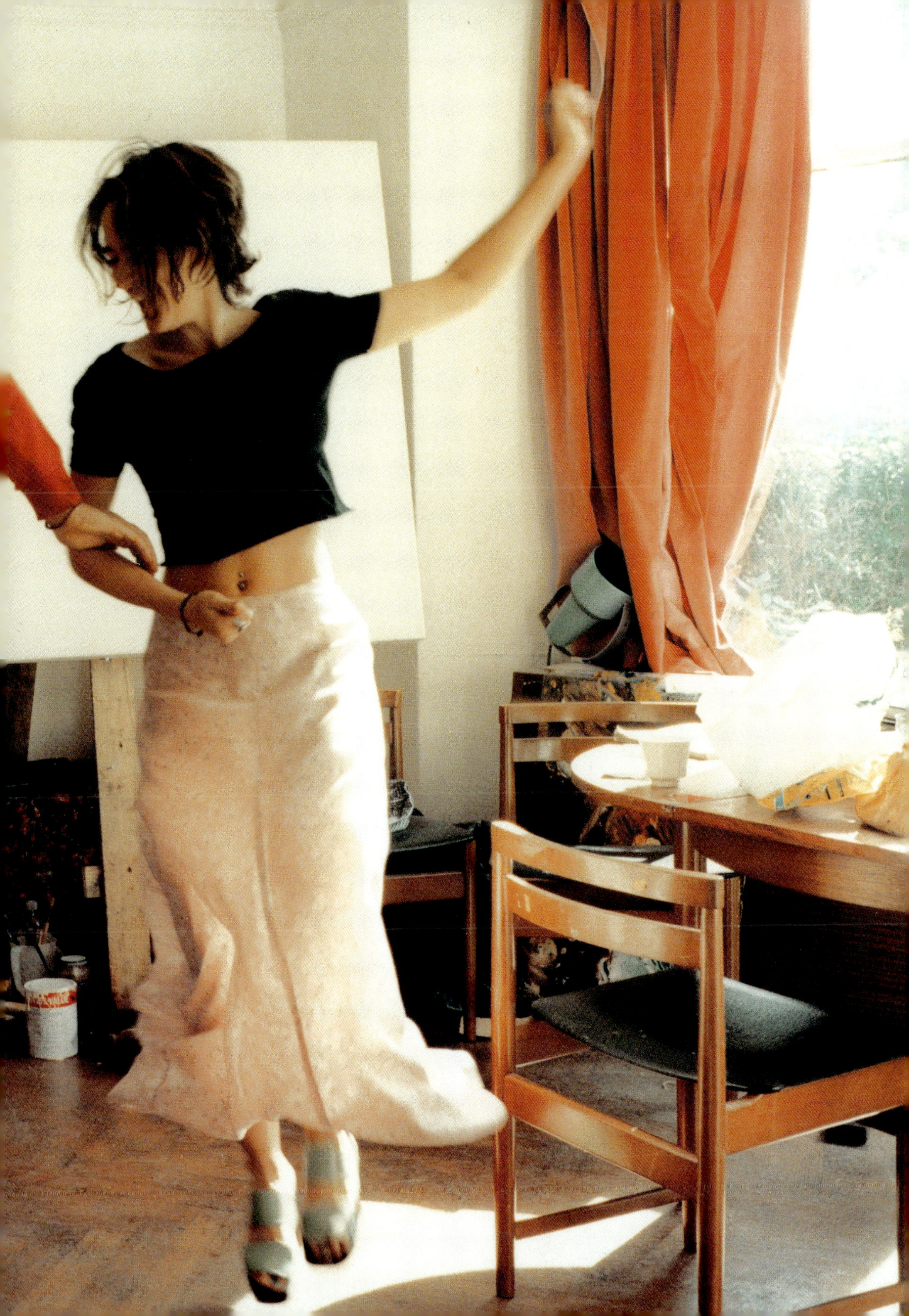

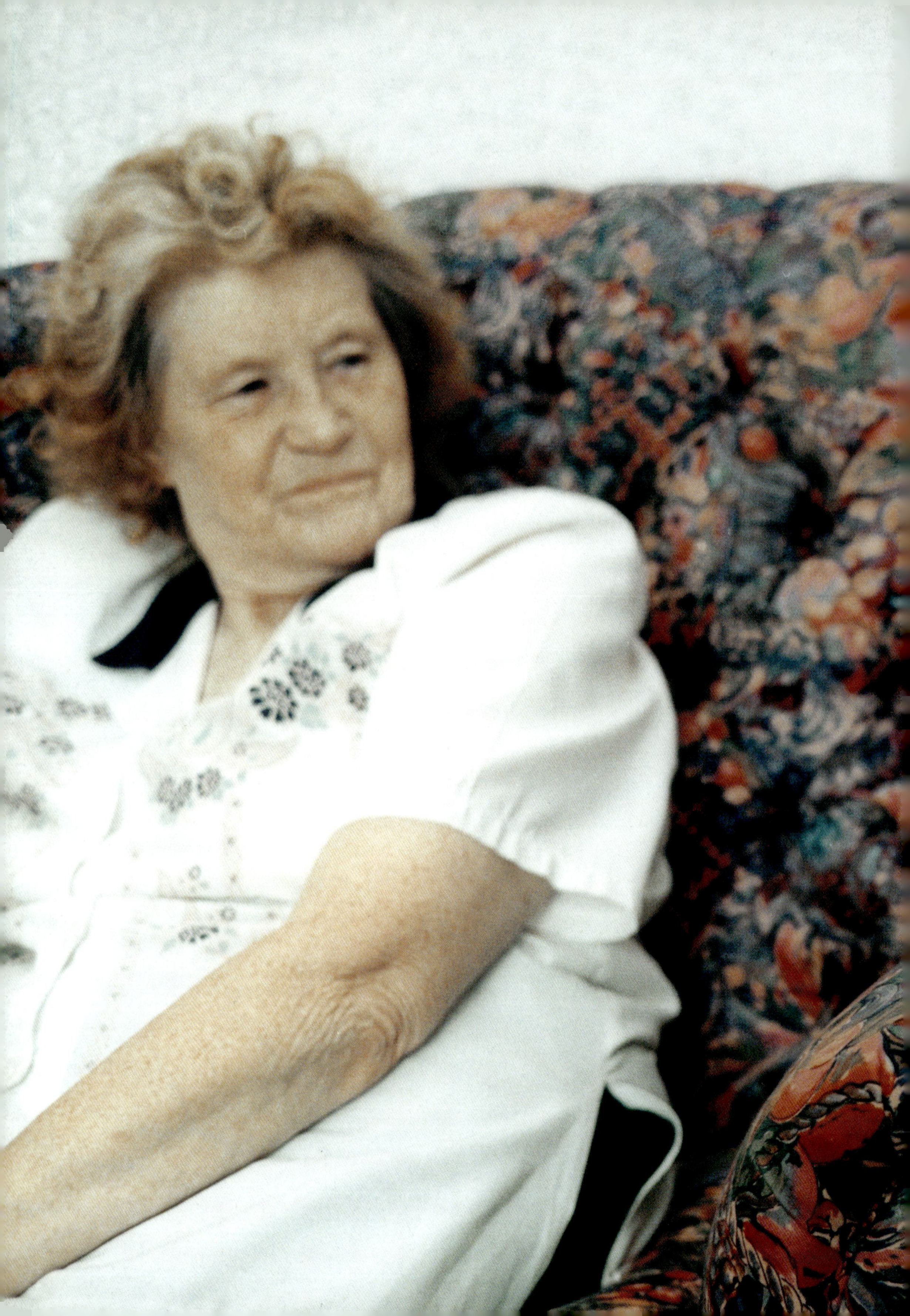

Poem for me Gran

The meat,
The meat,
Come see
The meat,
That's lovely
Isn't it
Frank?

J. Y.

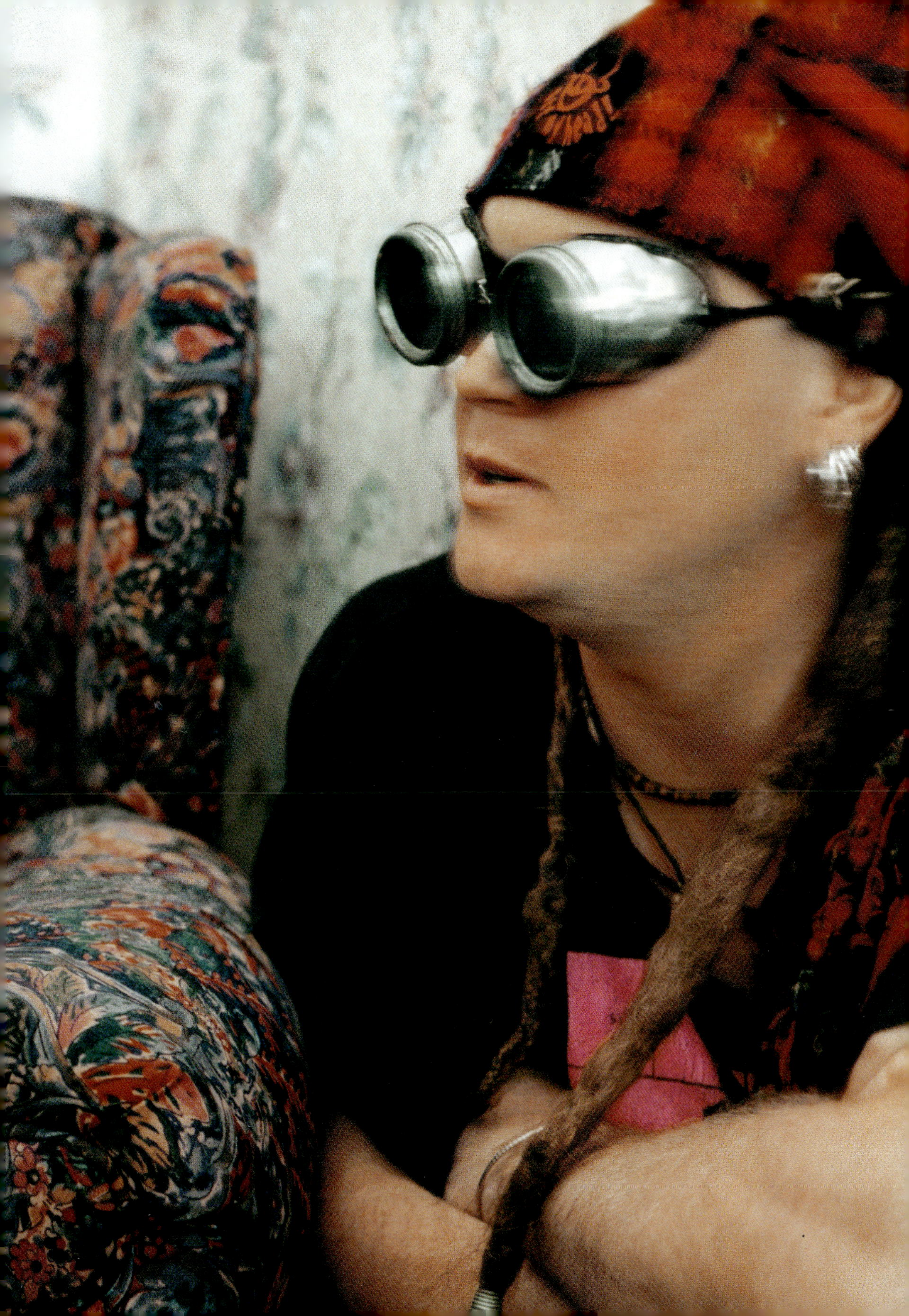

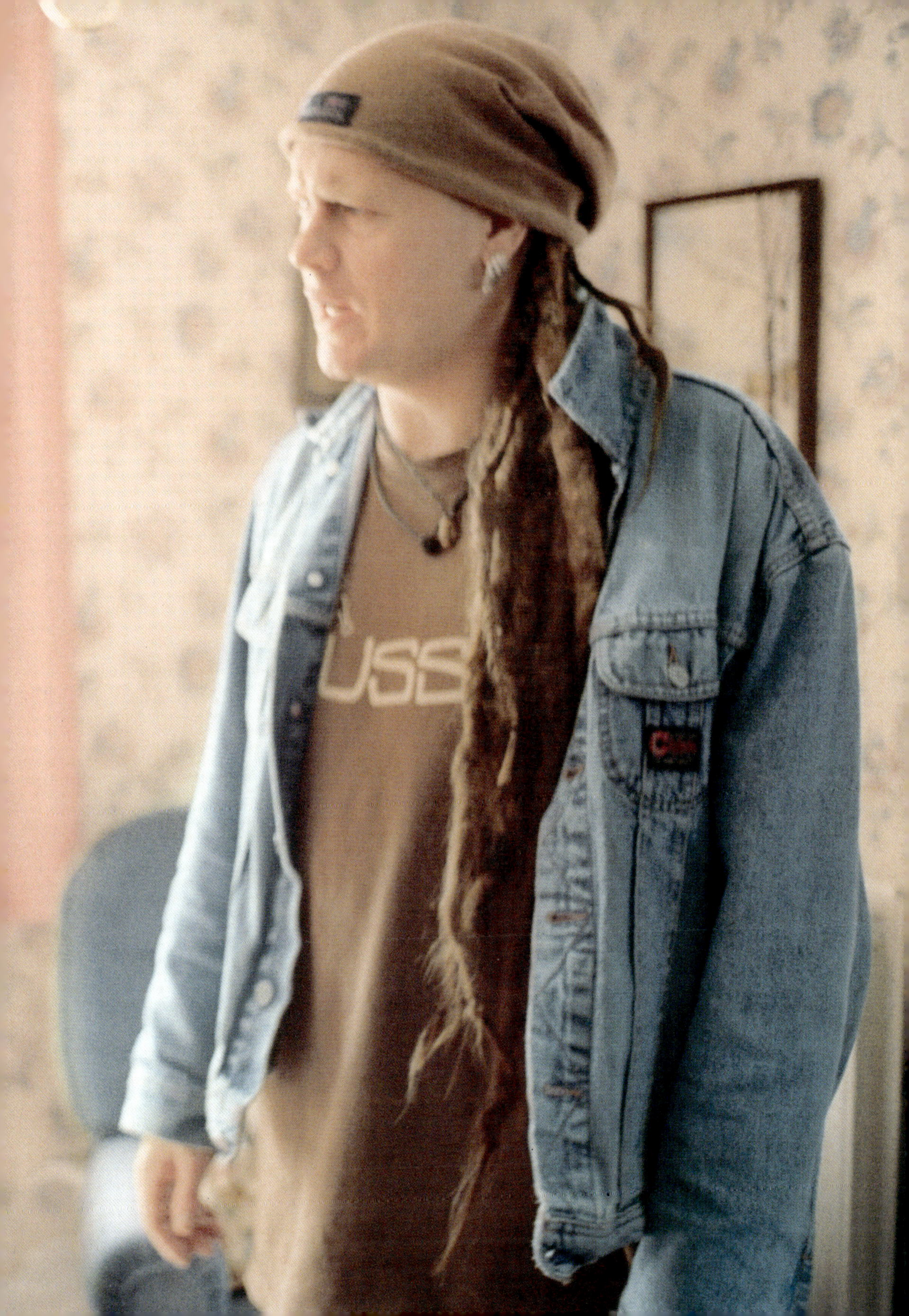

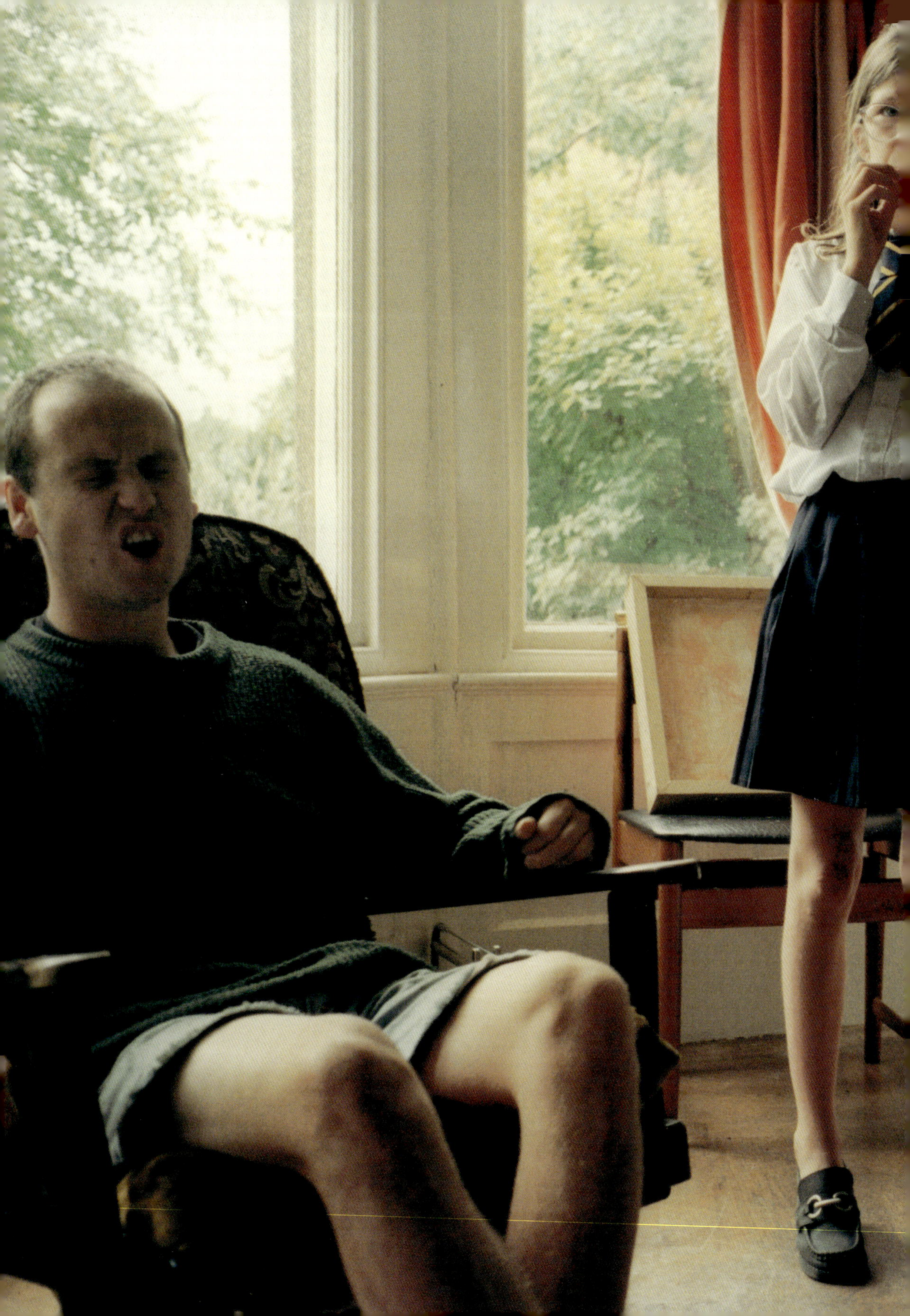

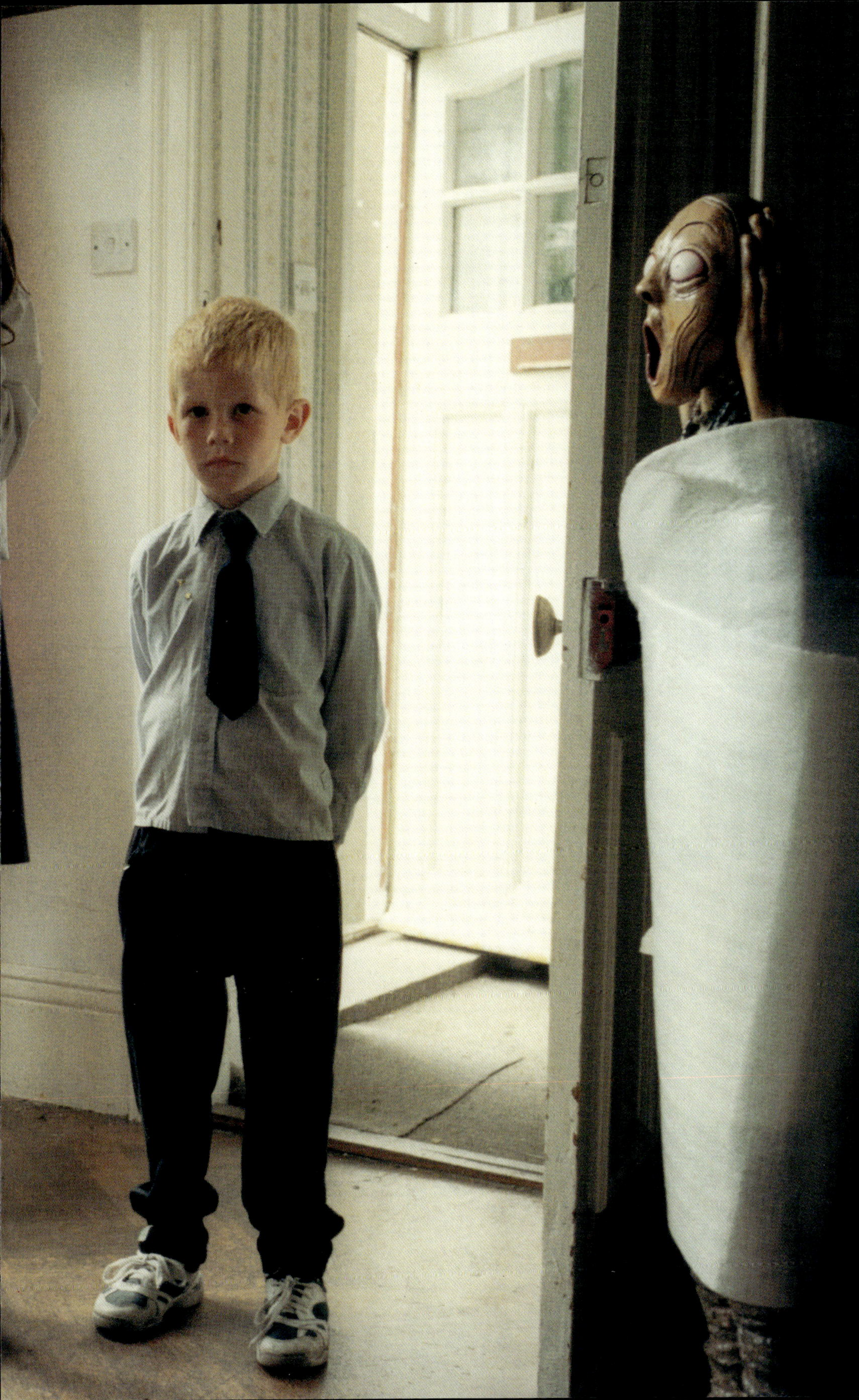

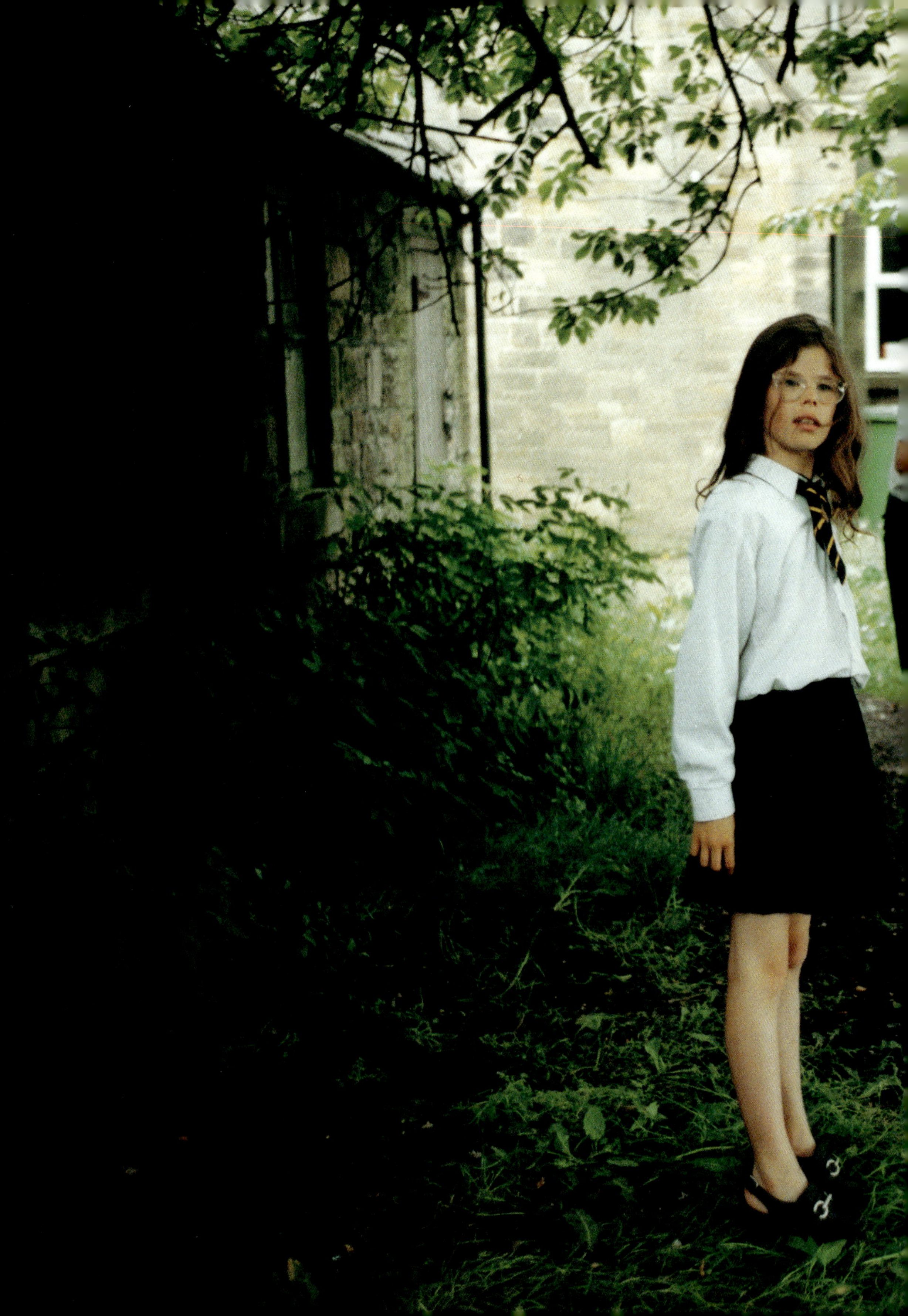

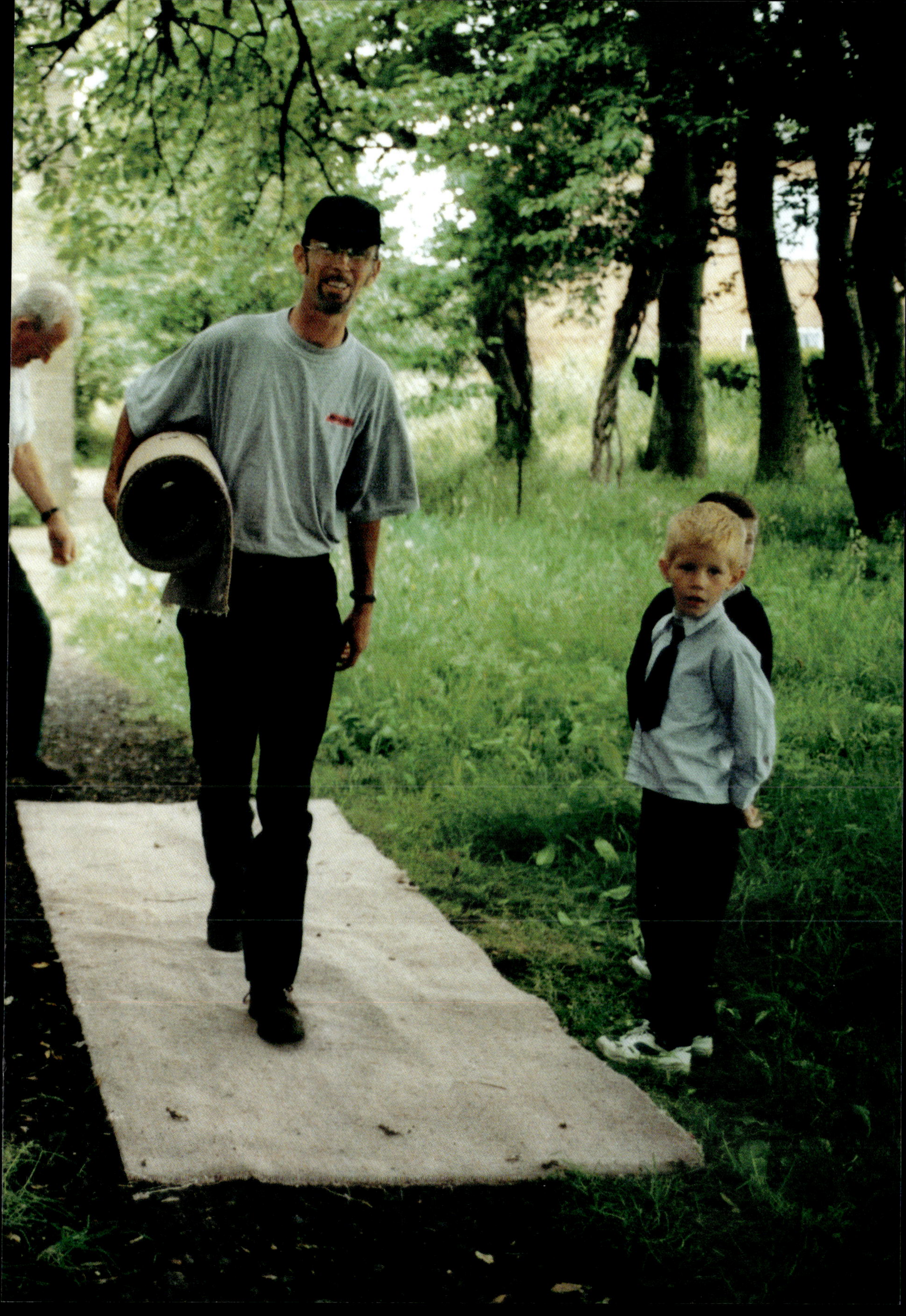

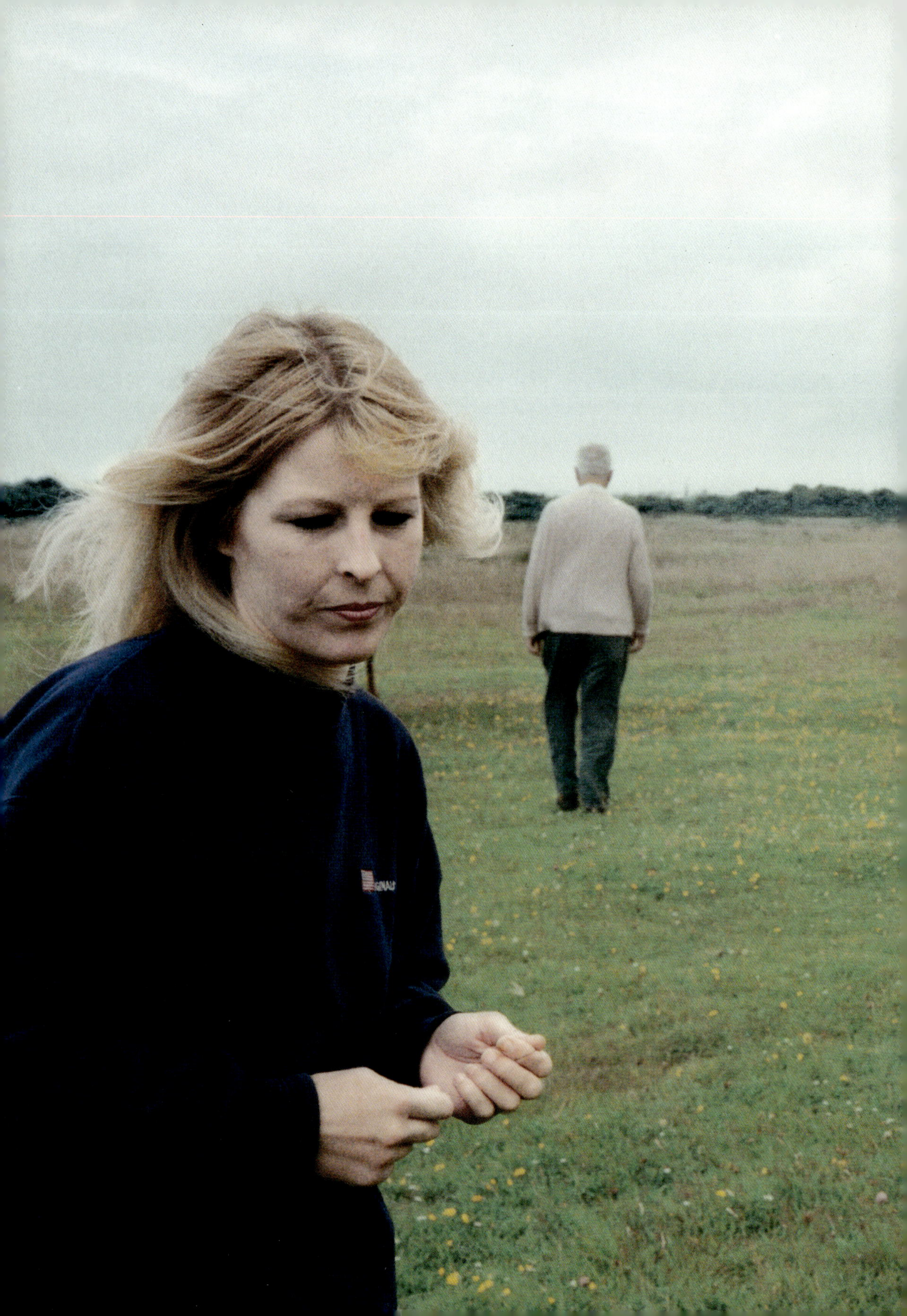

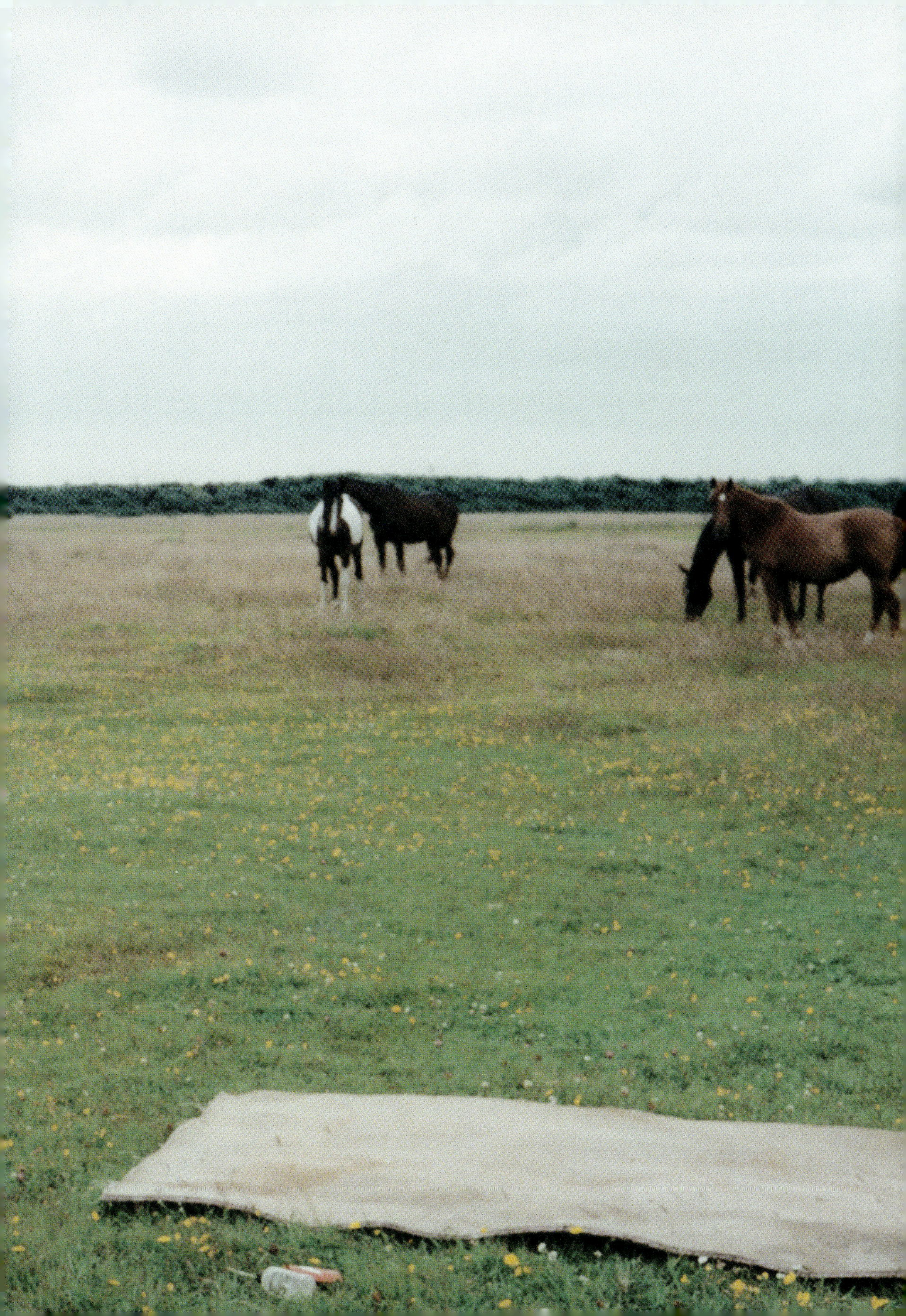

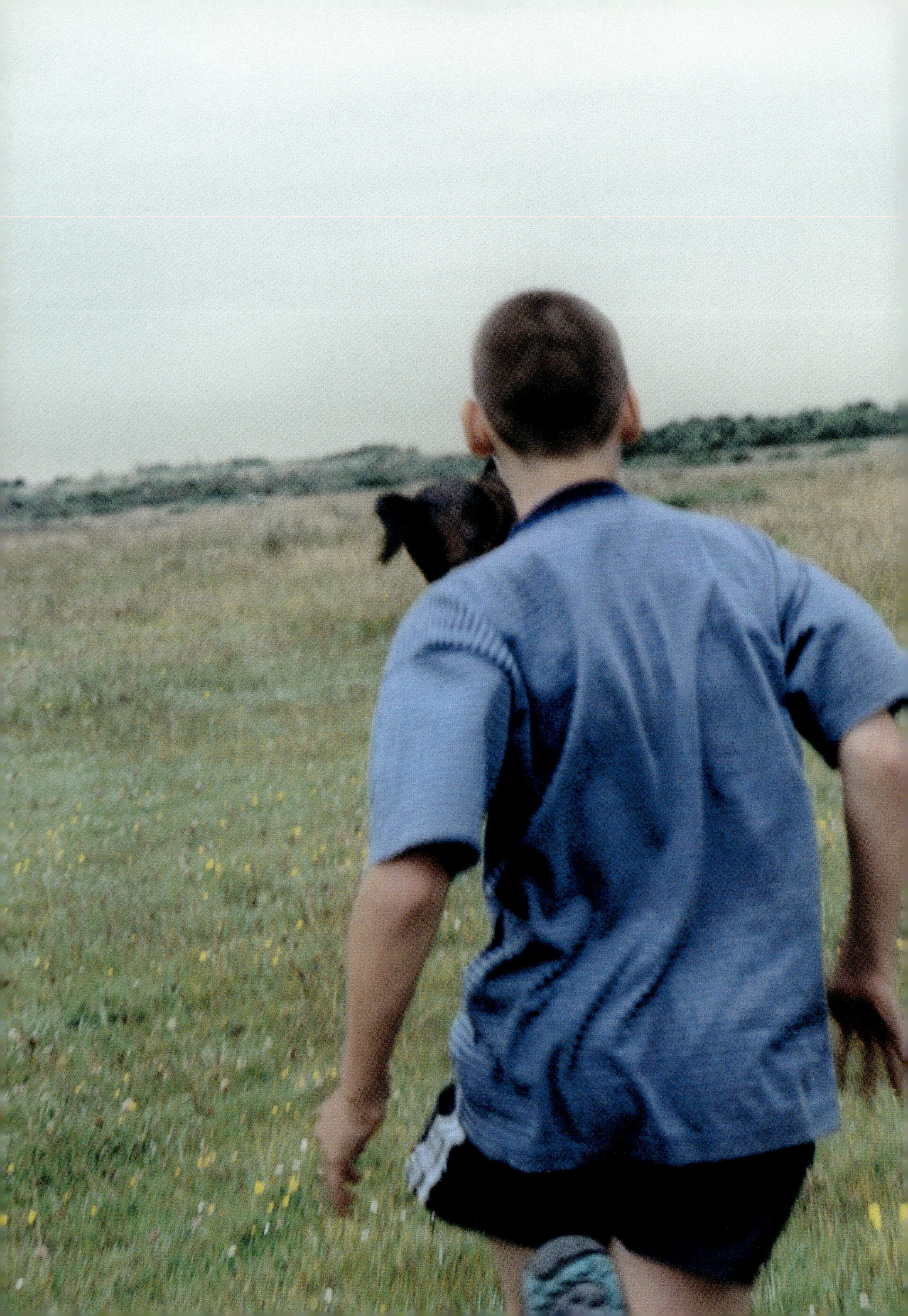

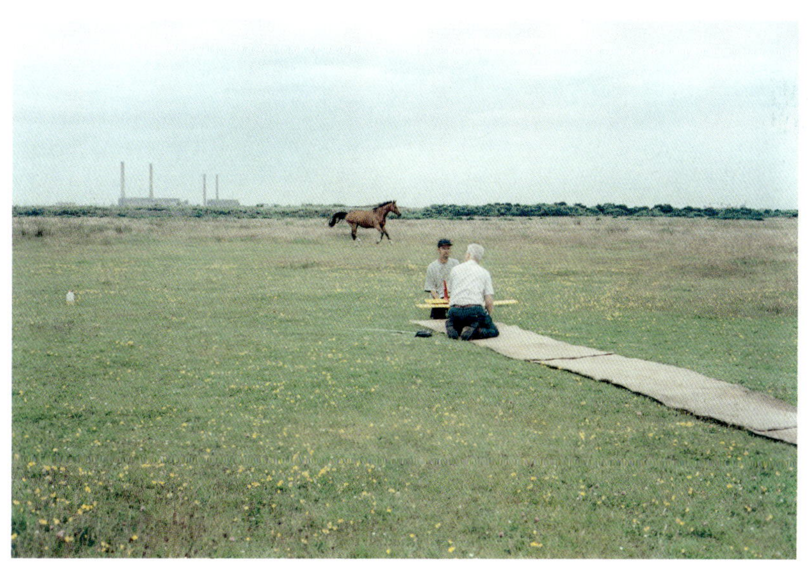

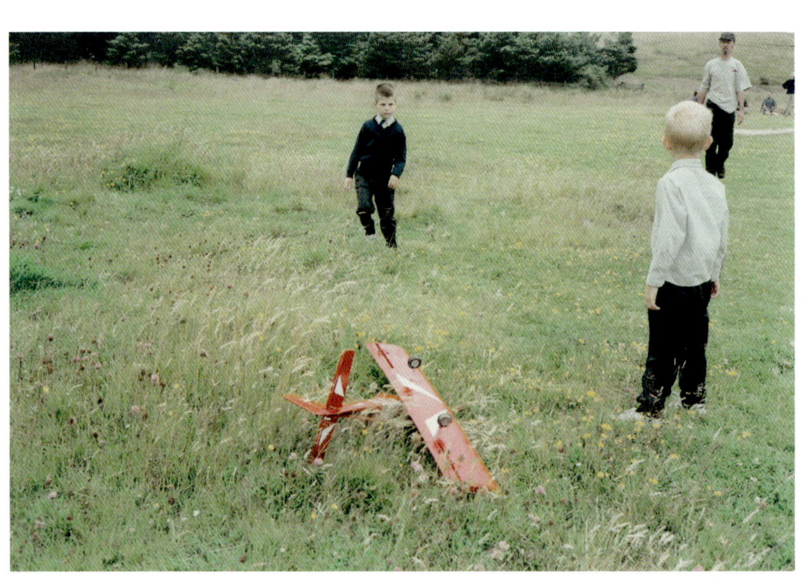

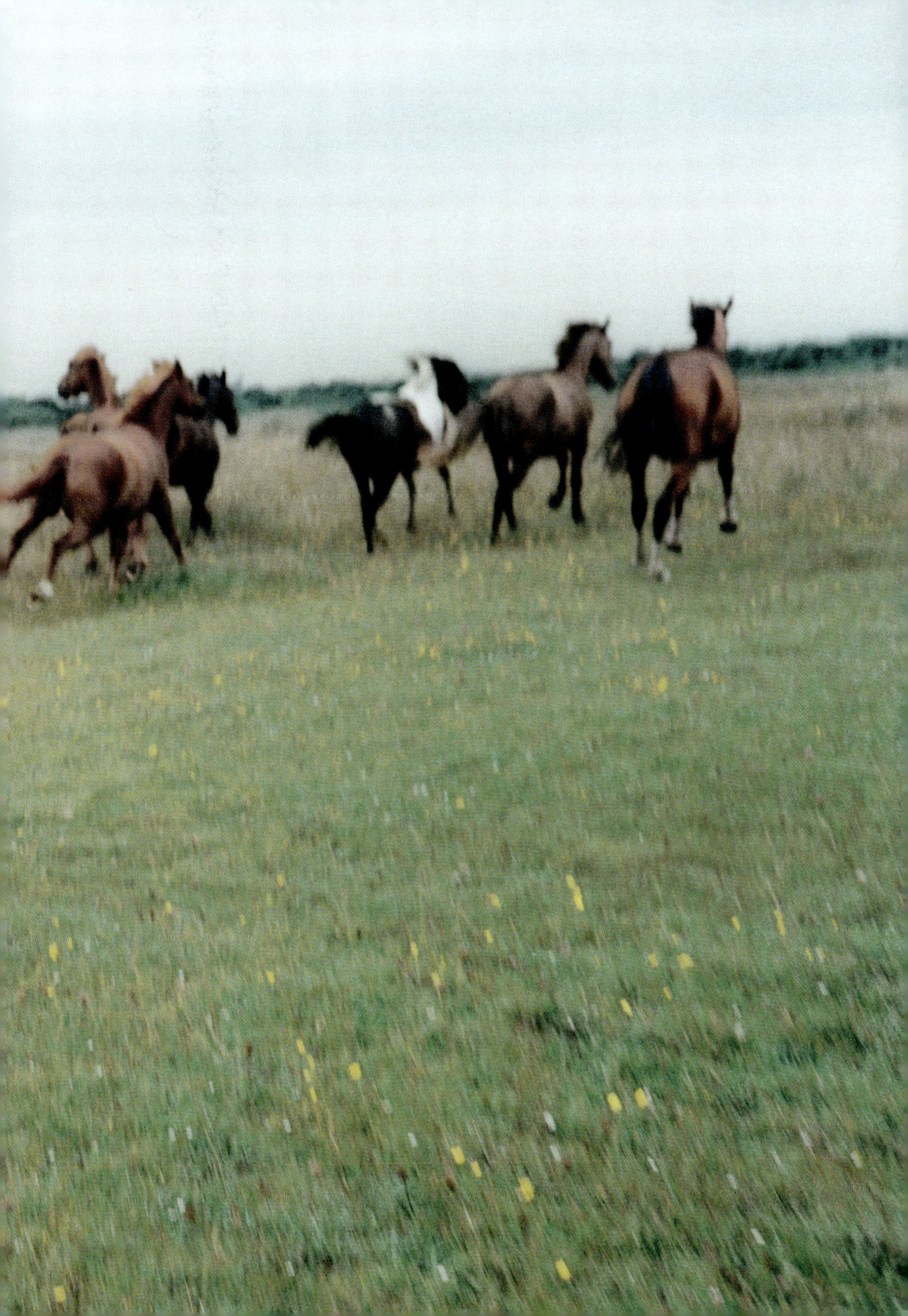

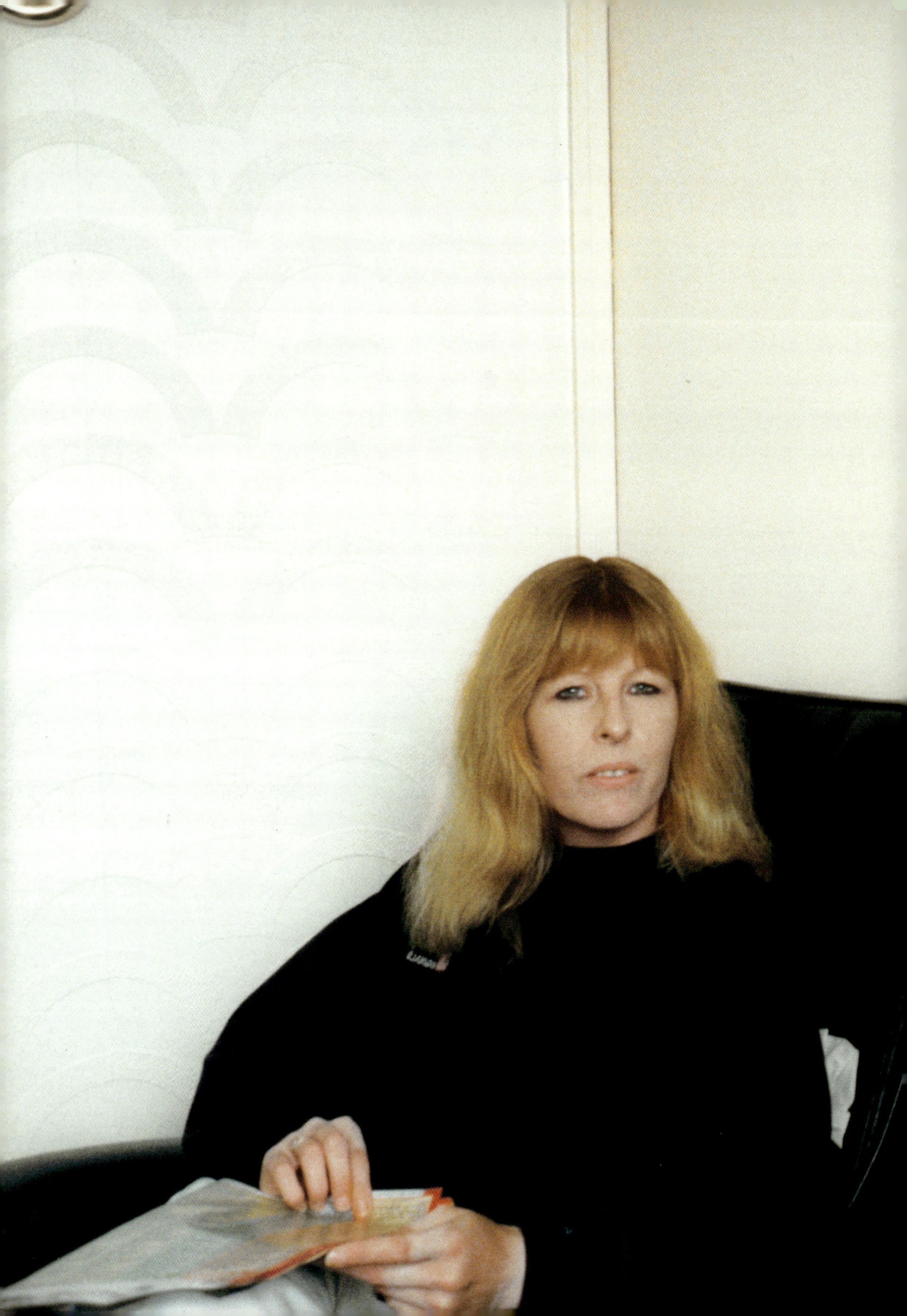

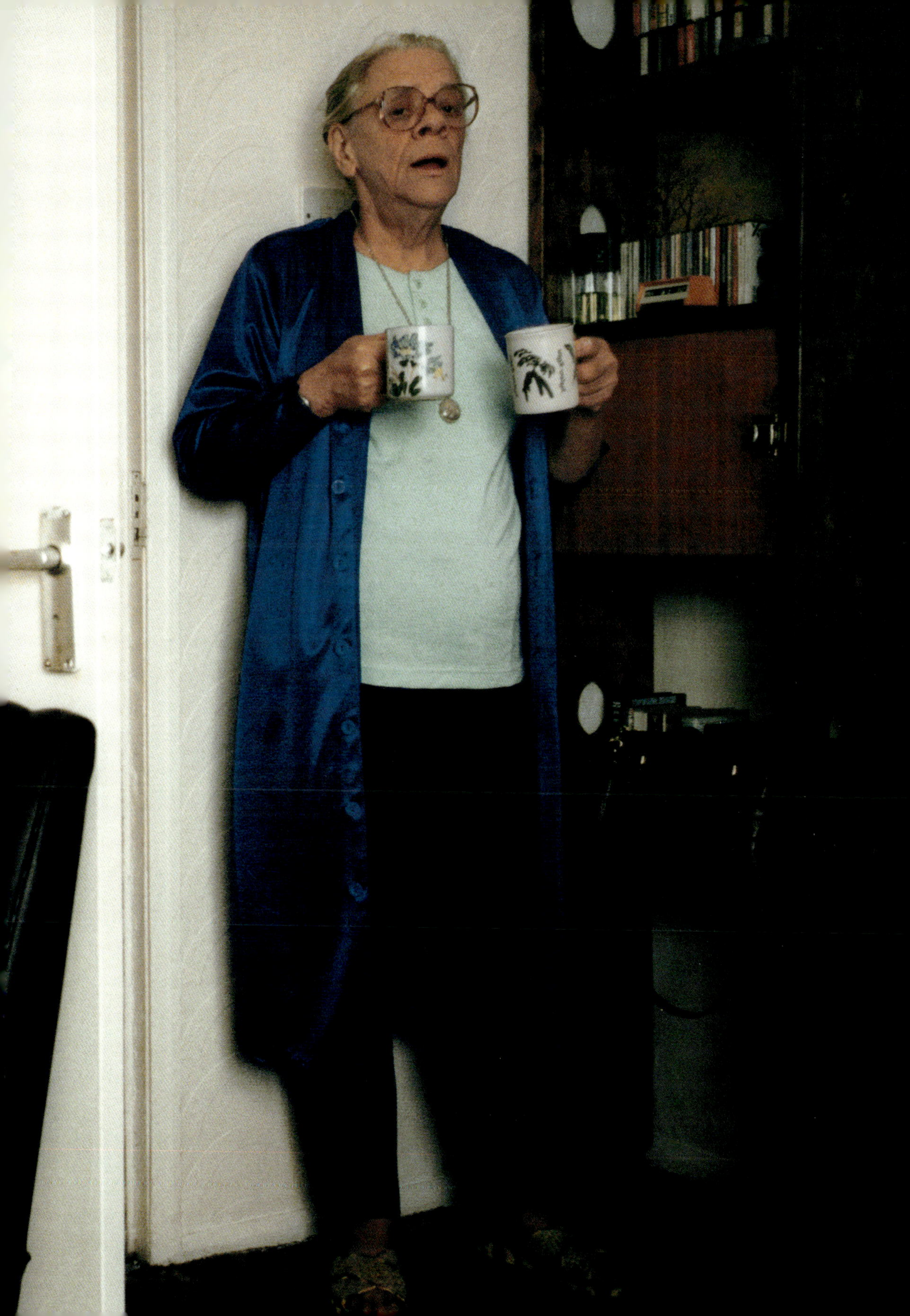

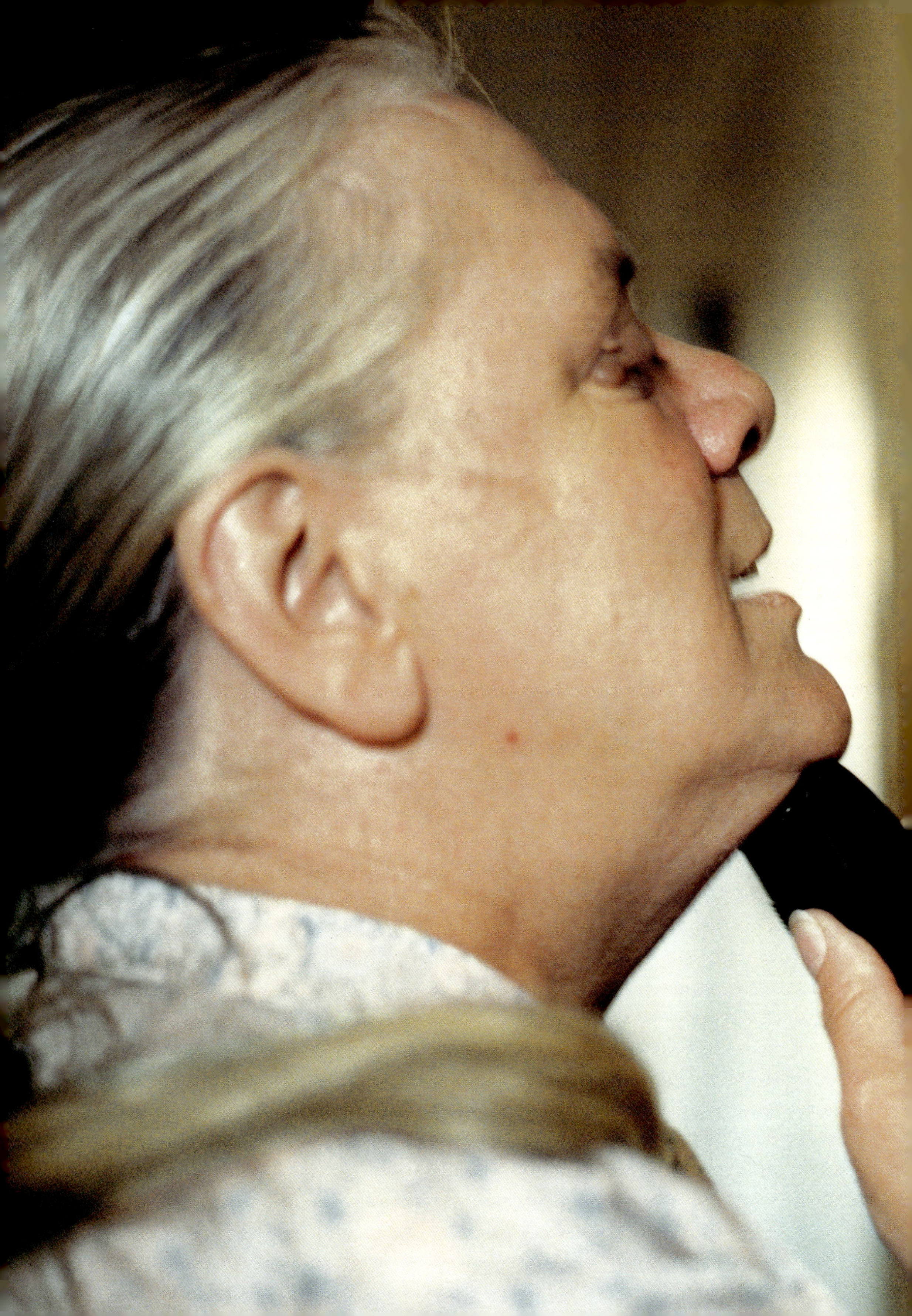

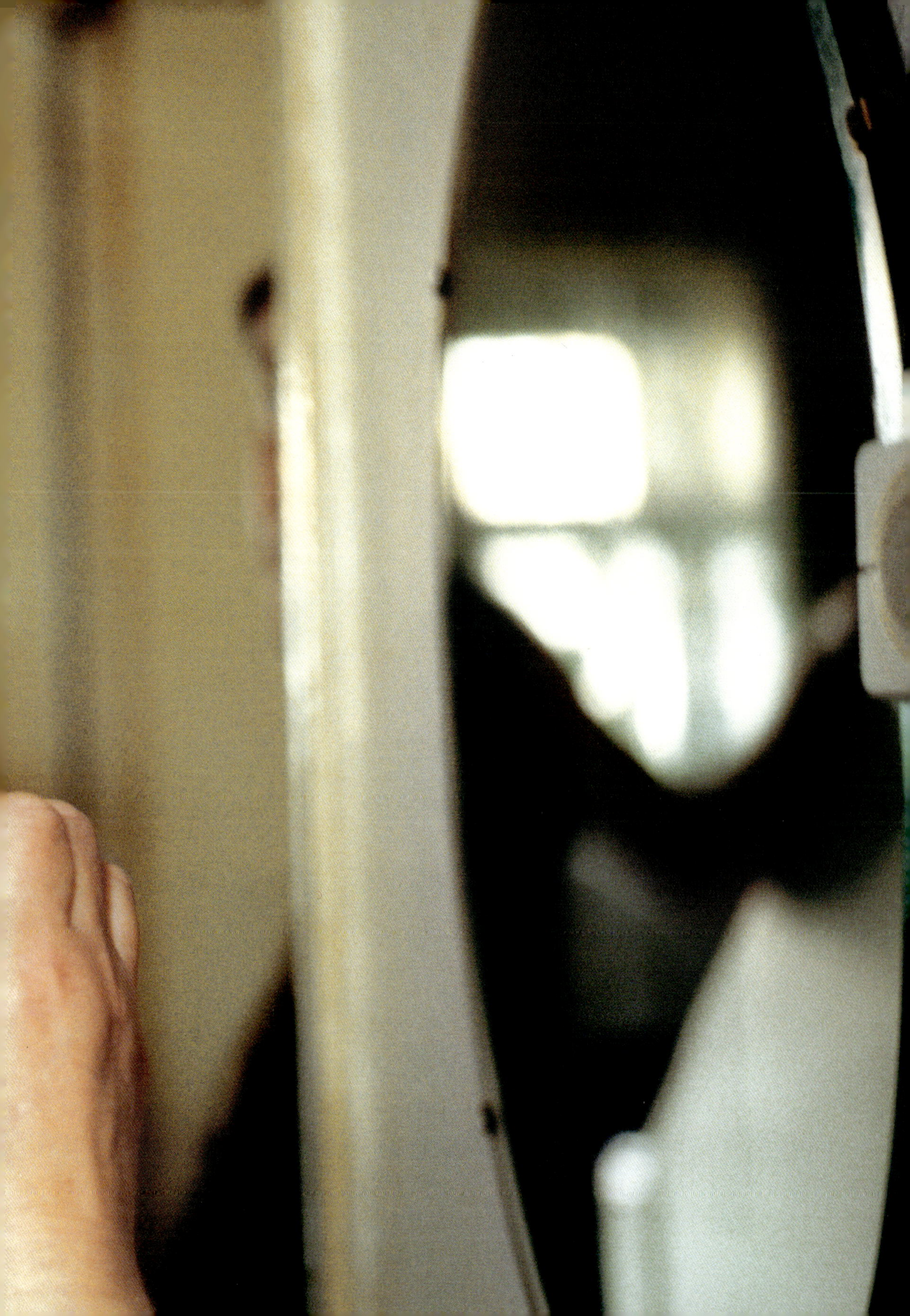

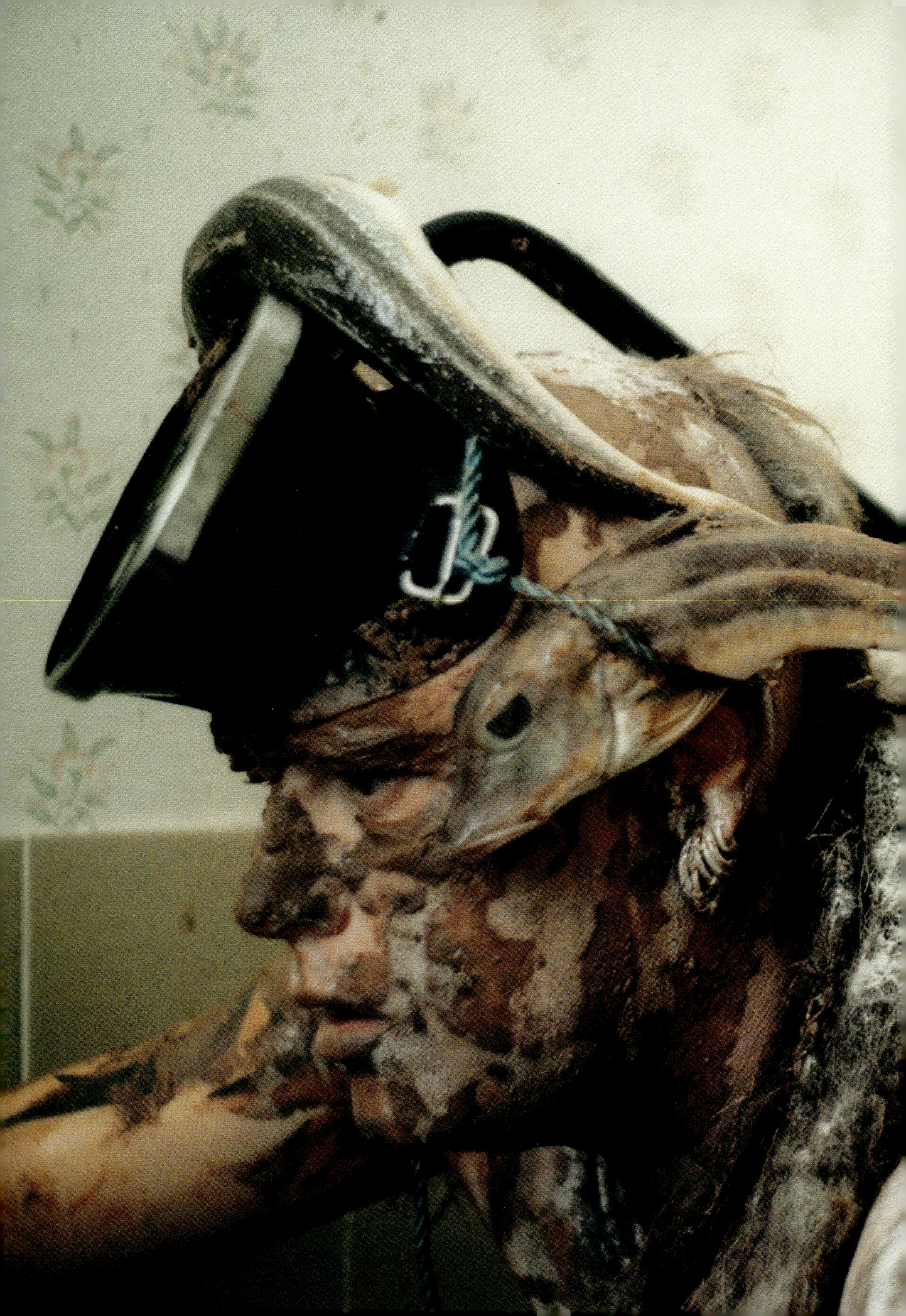

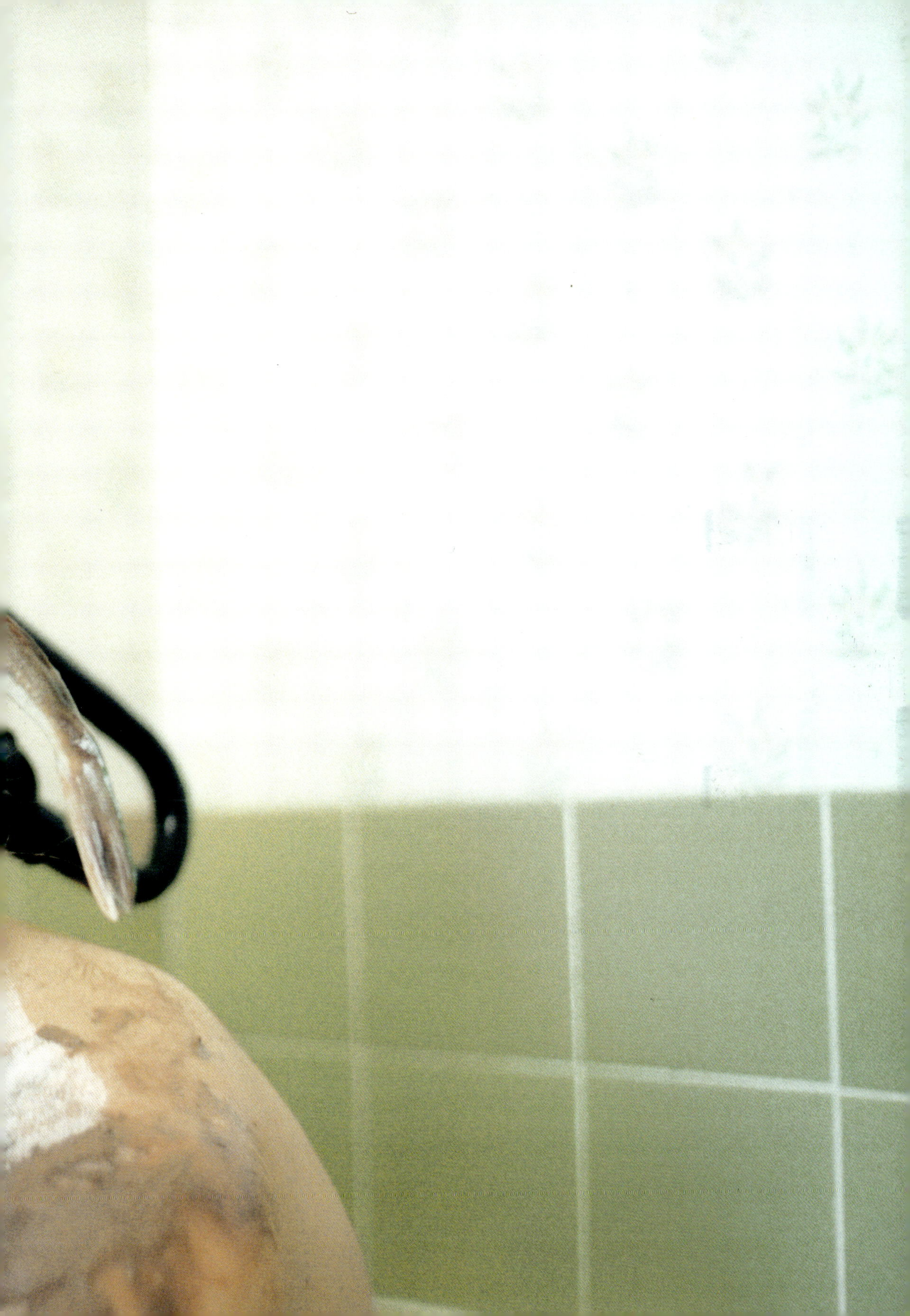

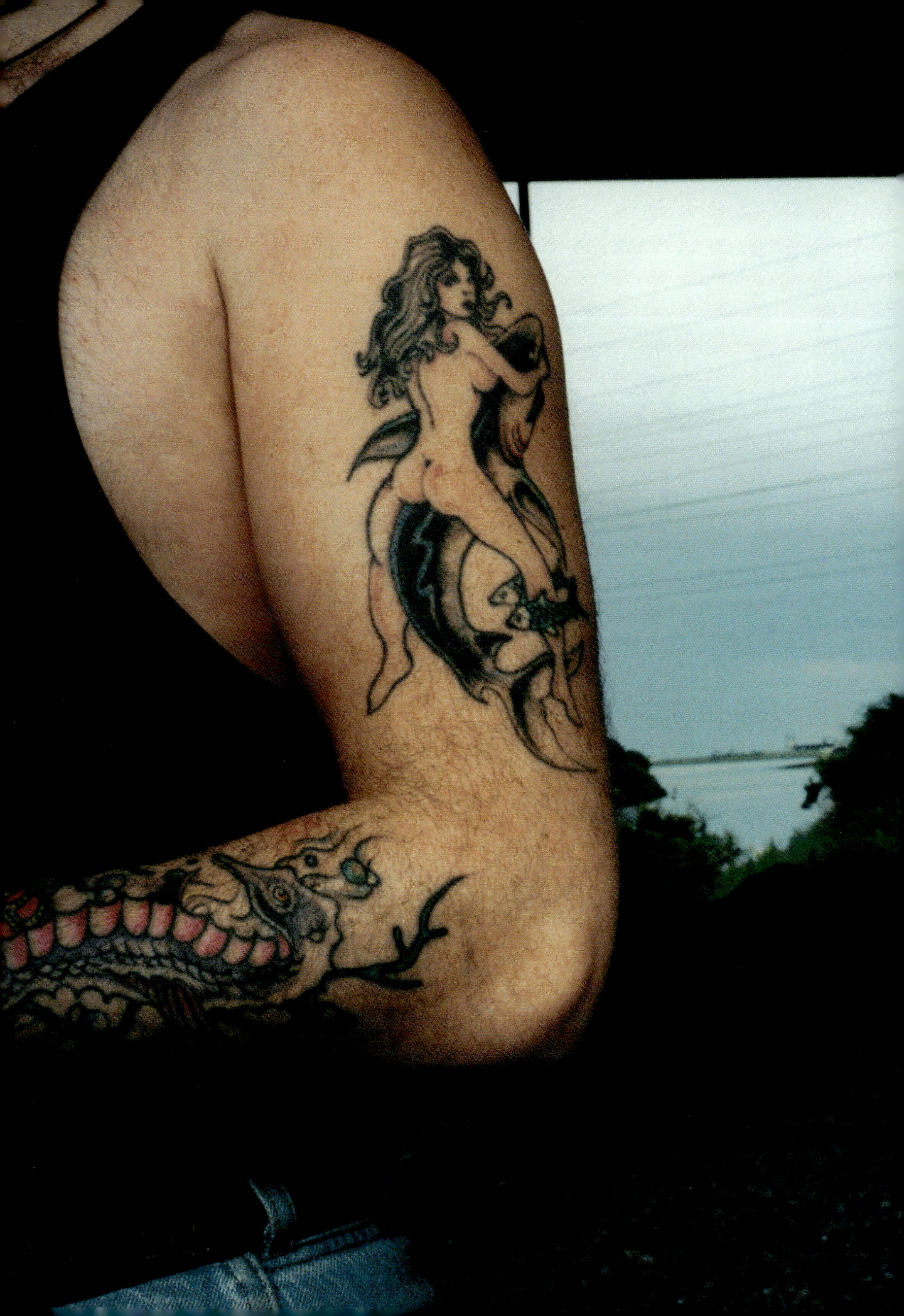

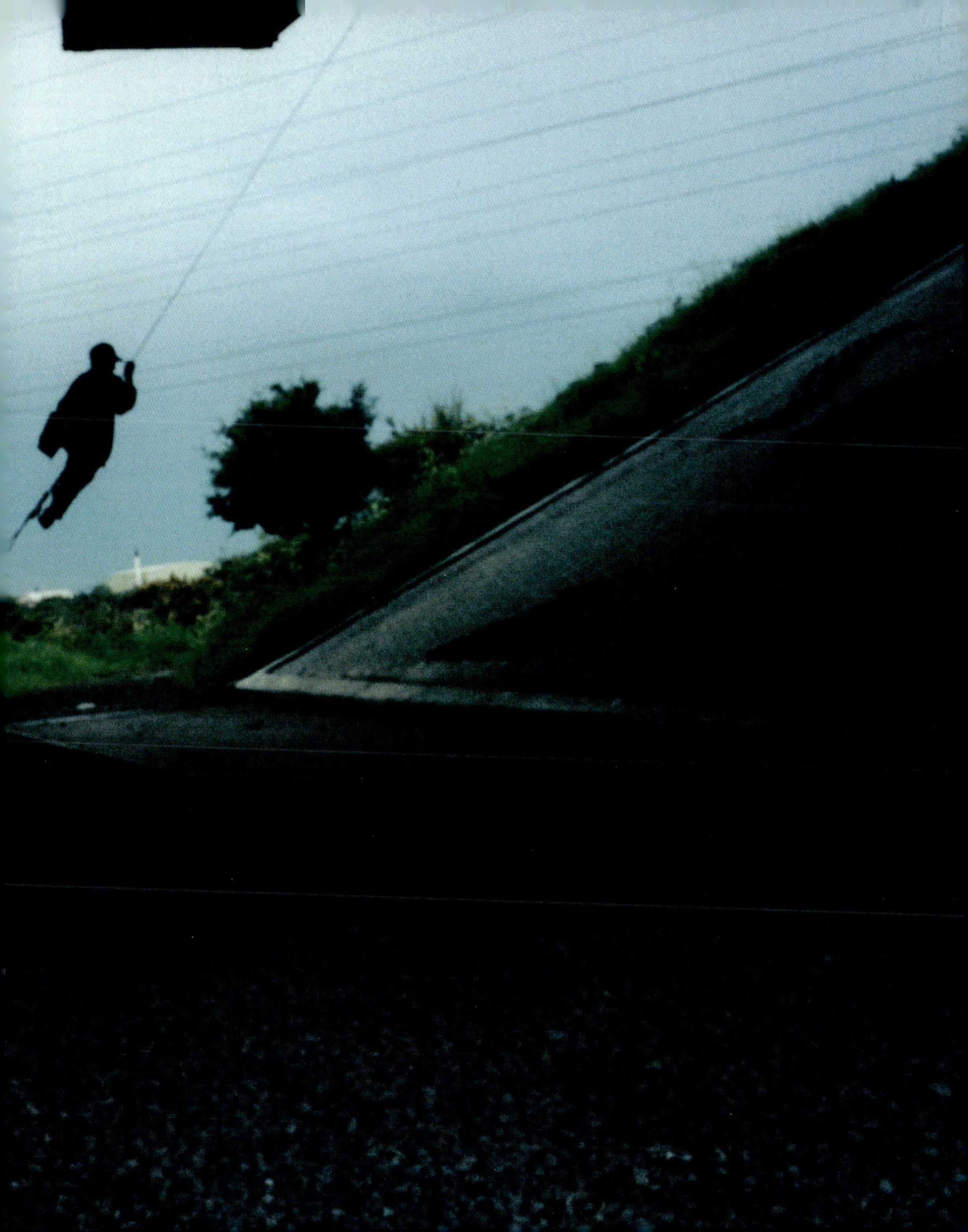

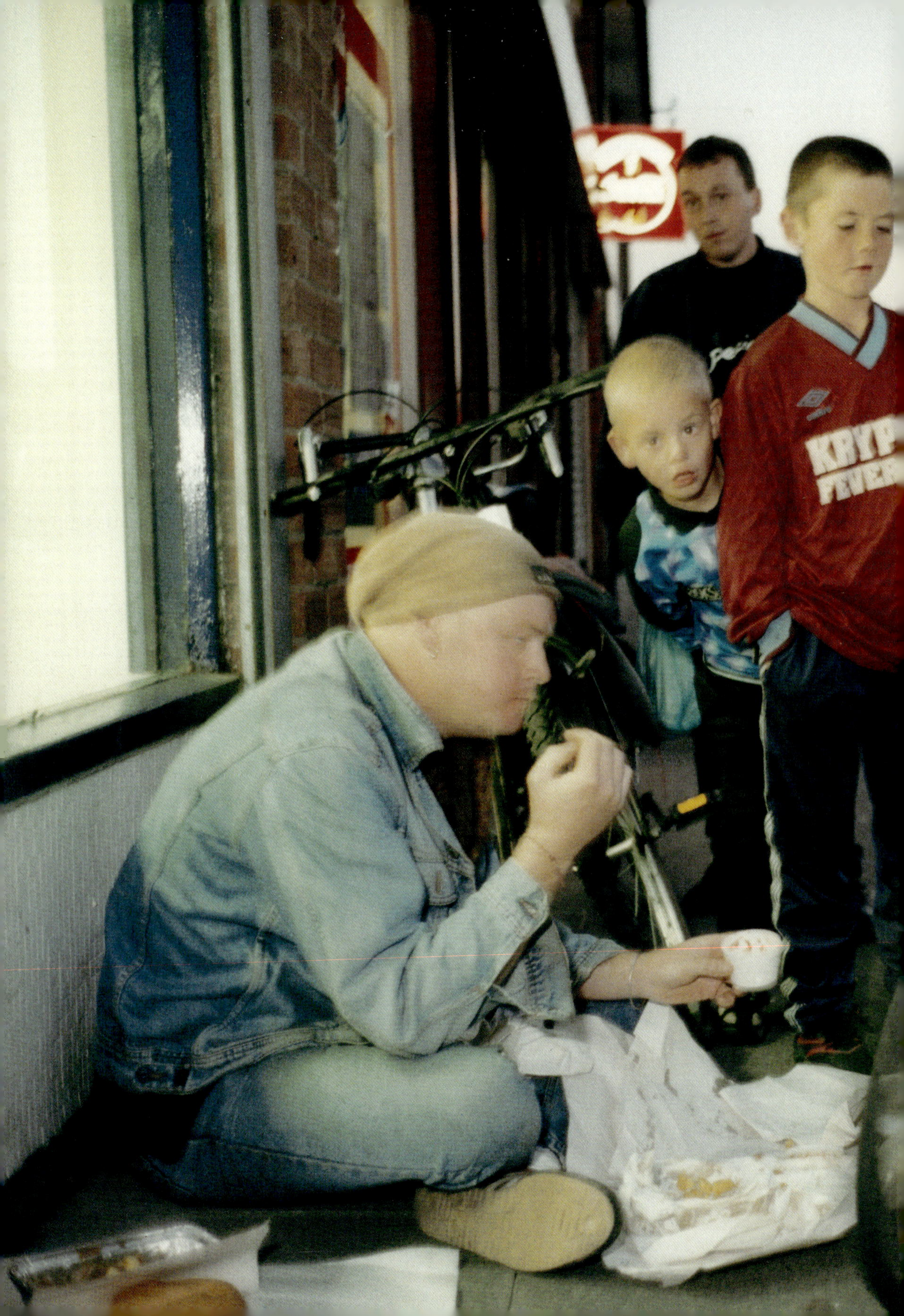
KRYP
FEVER

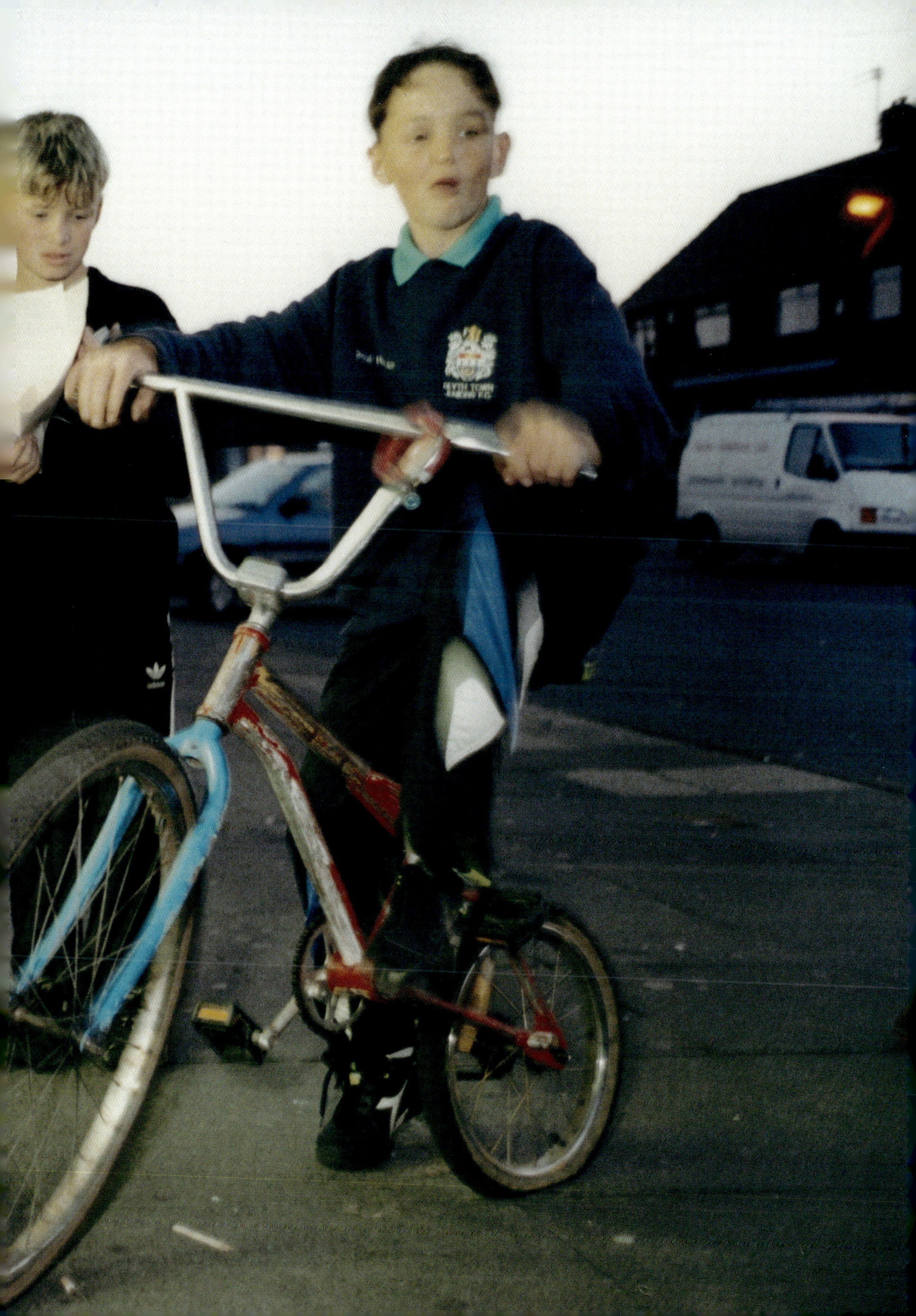

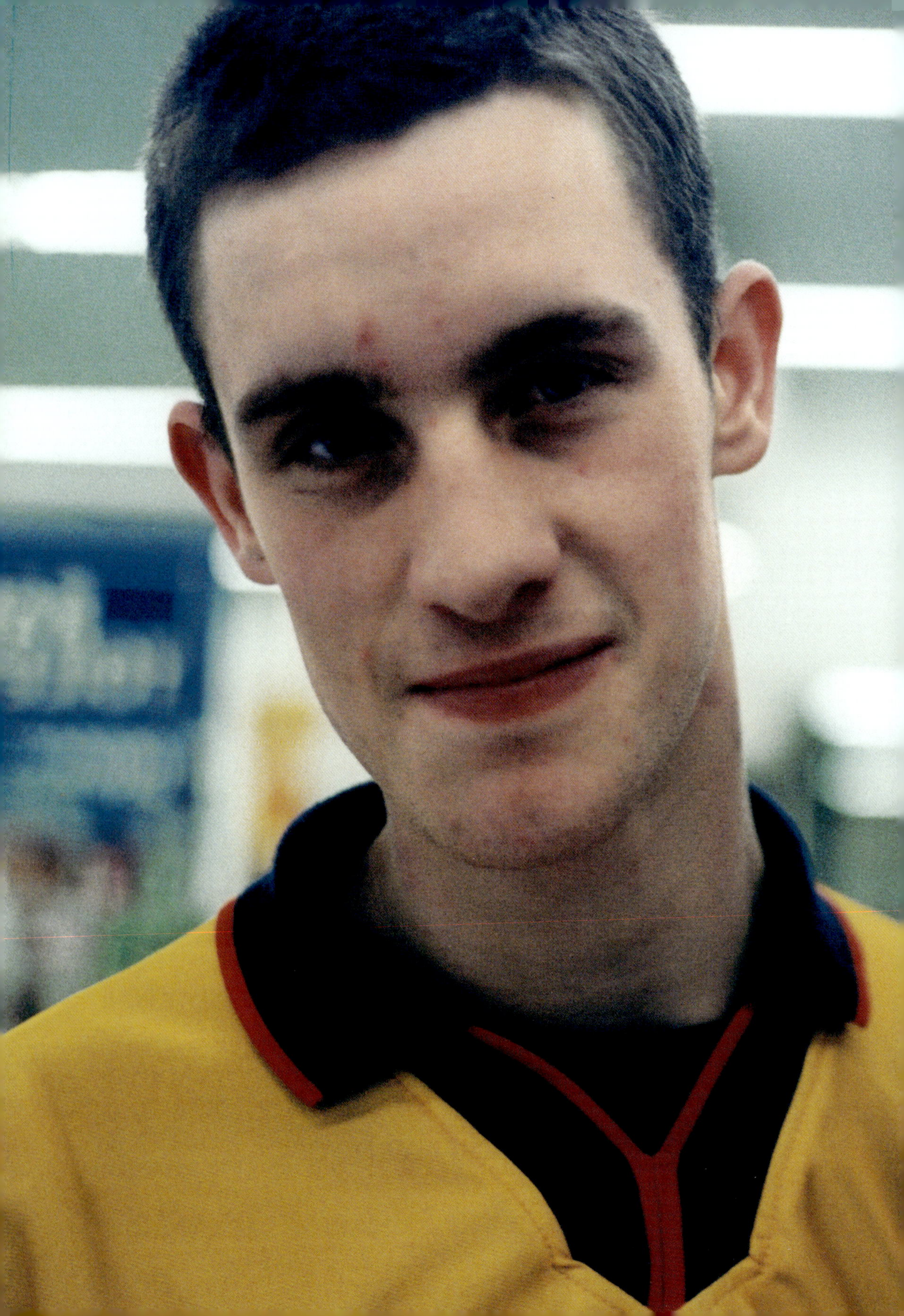

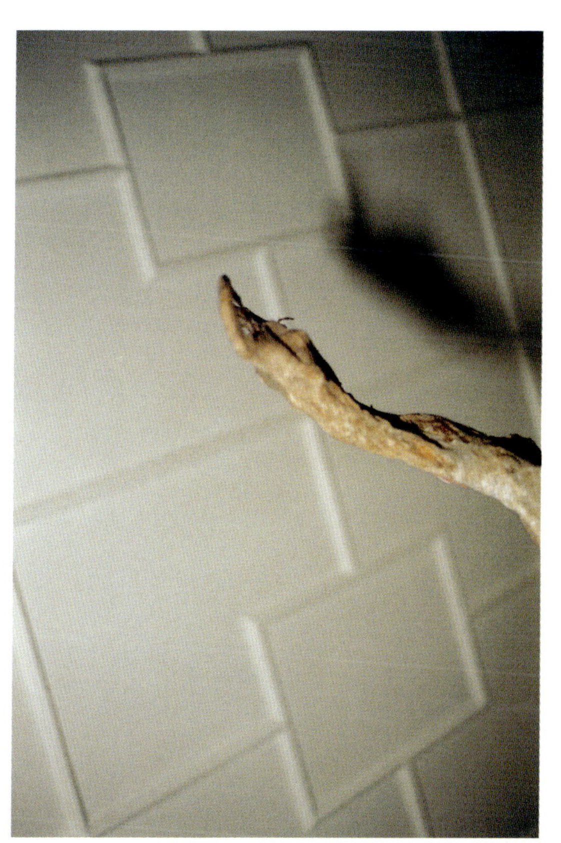

Have you seen her?
When she smiles,
Her teeth are manky.
That would make me sick.
That's enough to put you off your dinner.

J. Y.

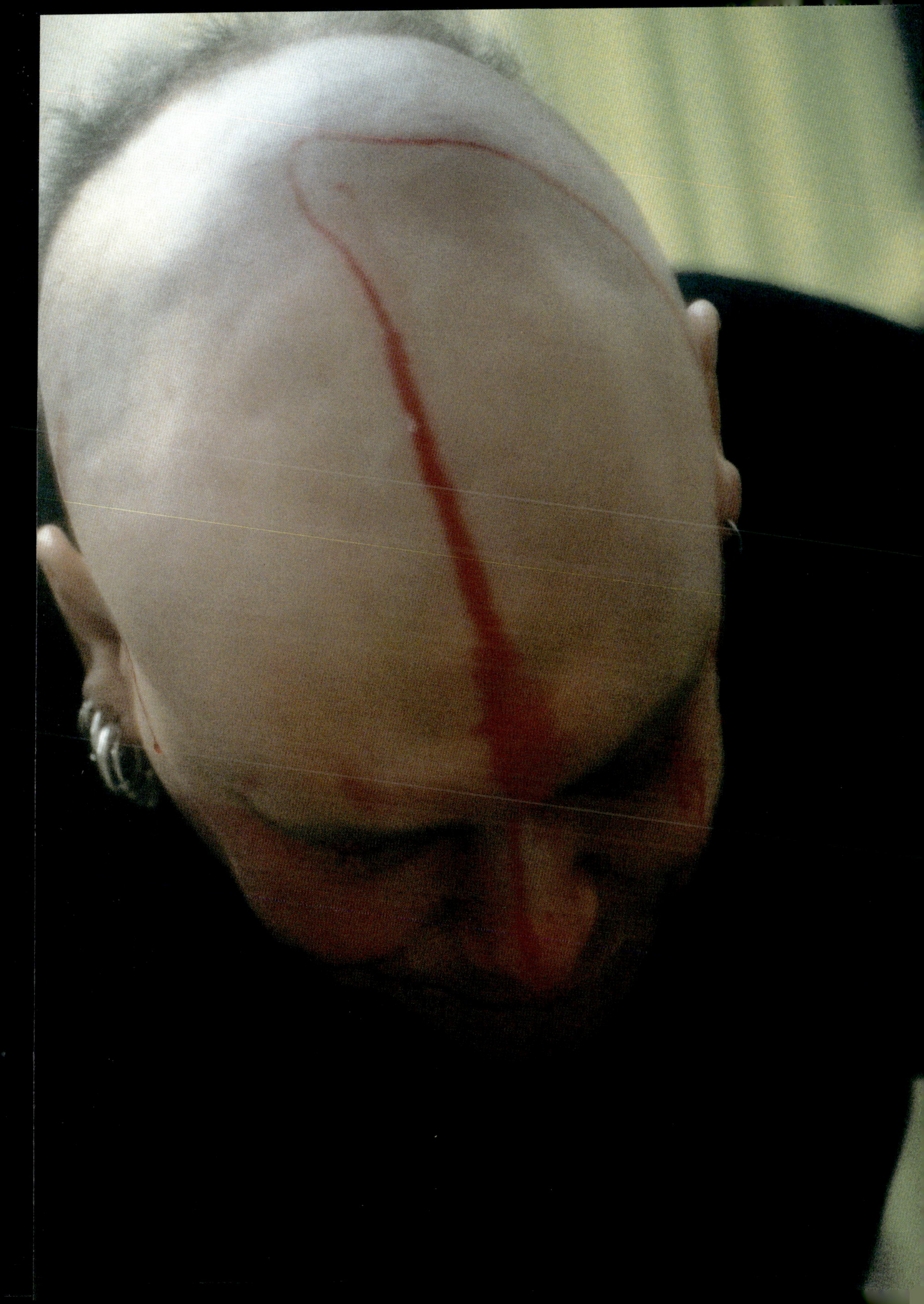

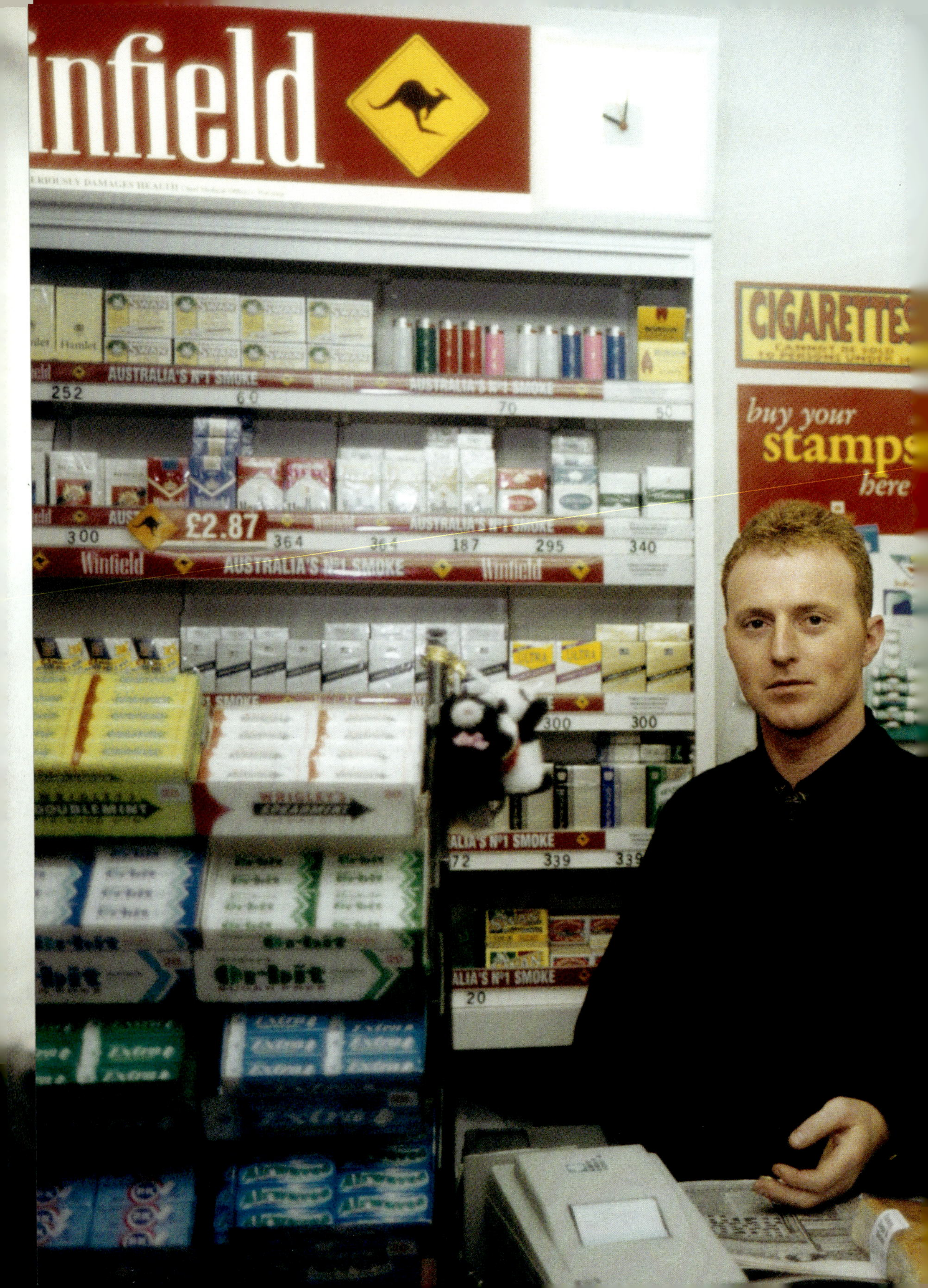

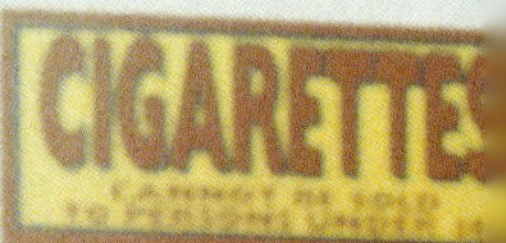
CIGARETTES

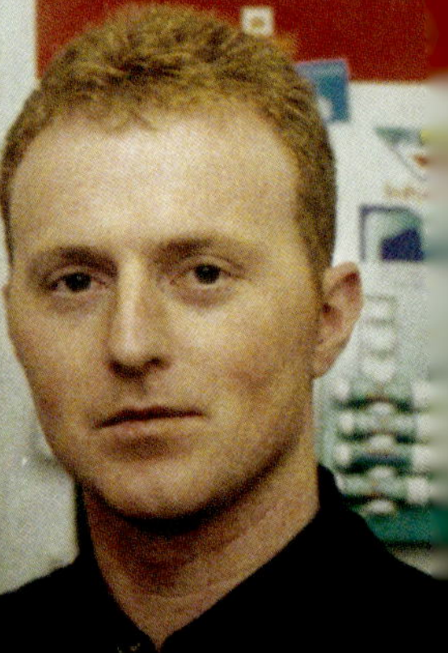
buy your
stamps
here

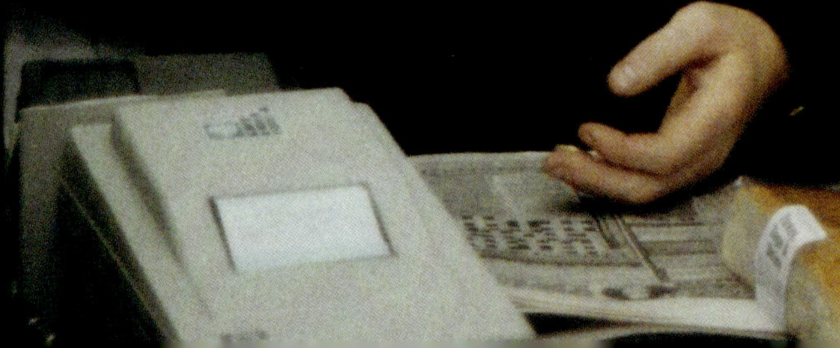

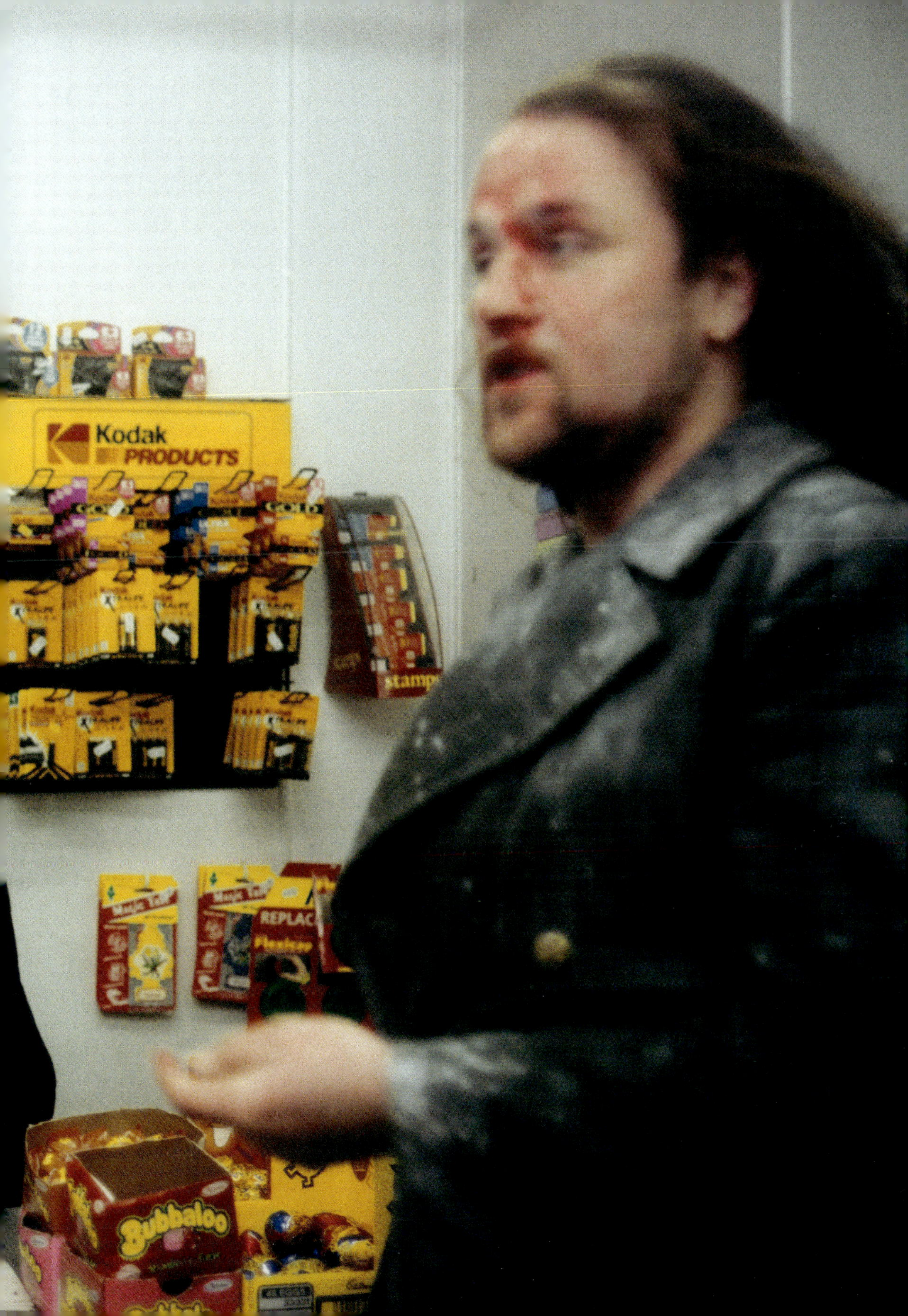
Kodak
PRODUCTS
Bubbaloo

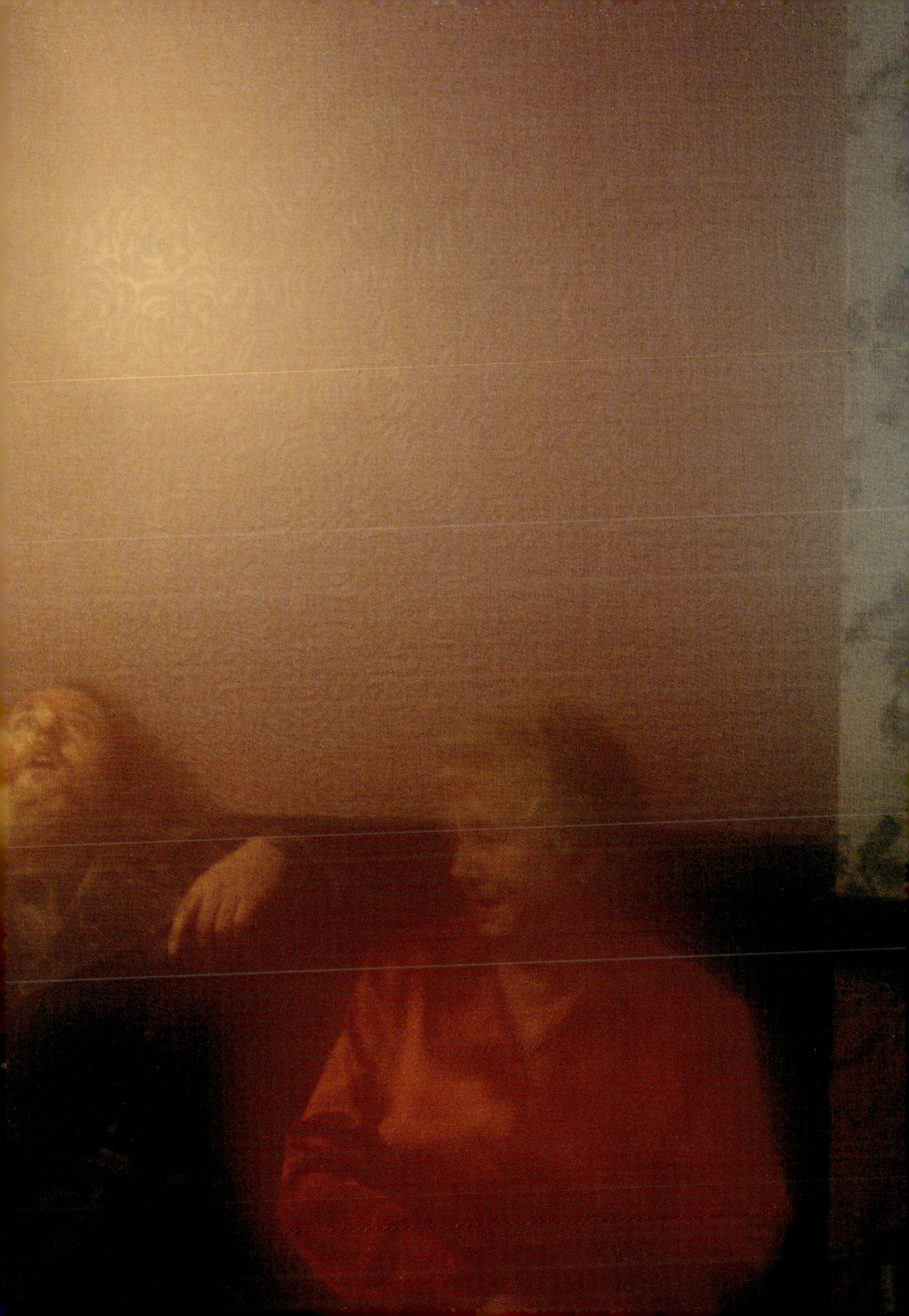

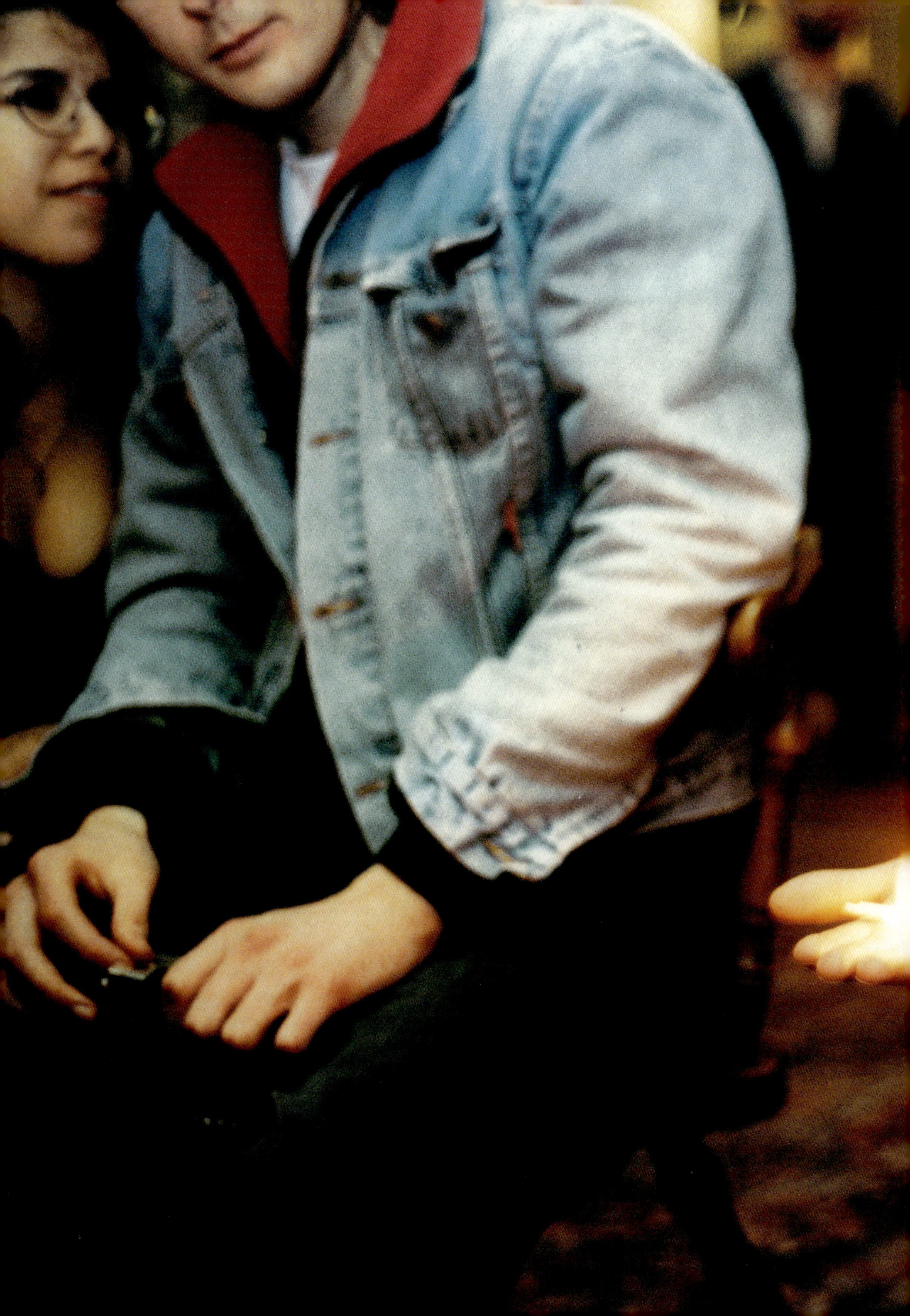

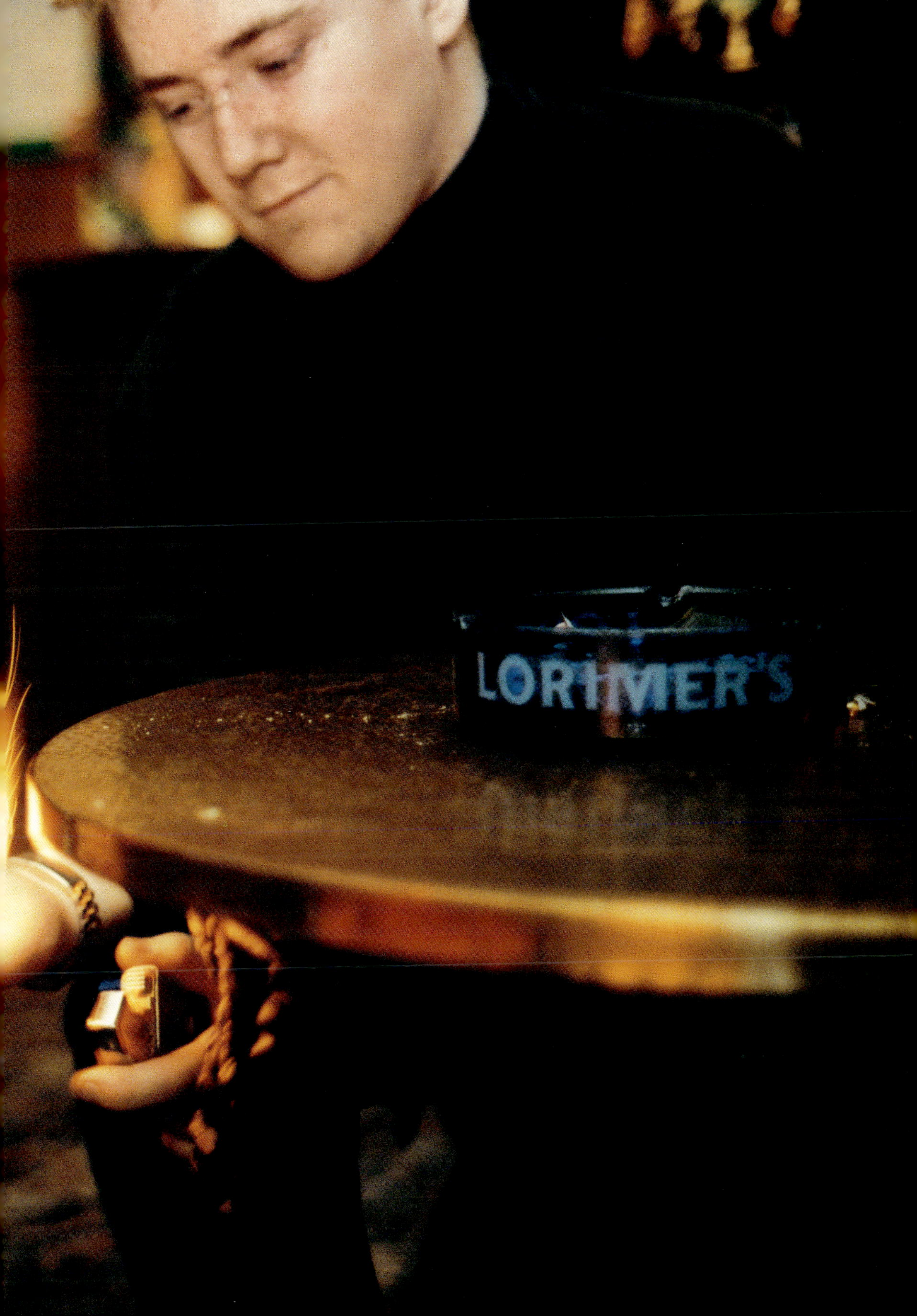
LORIMER'S

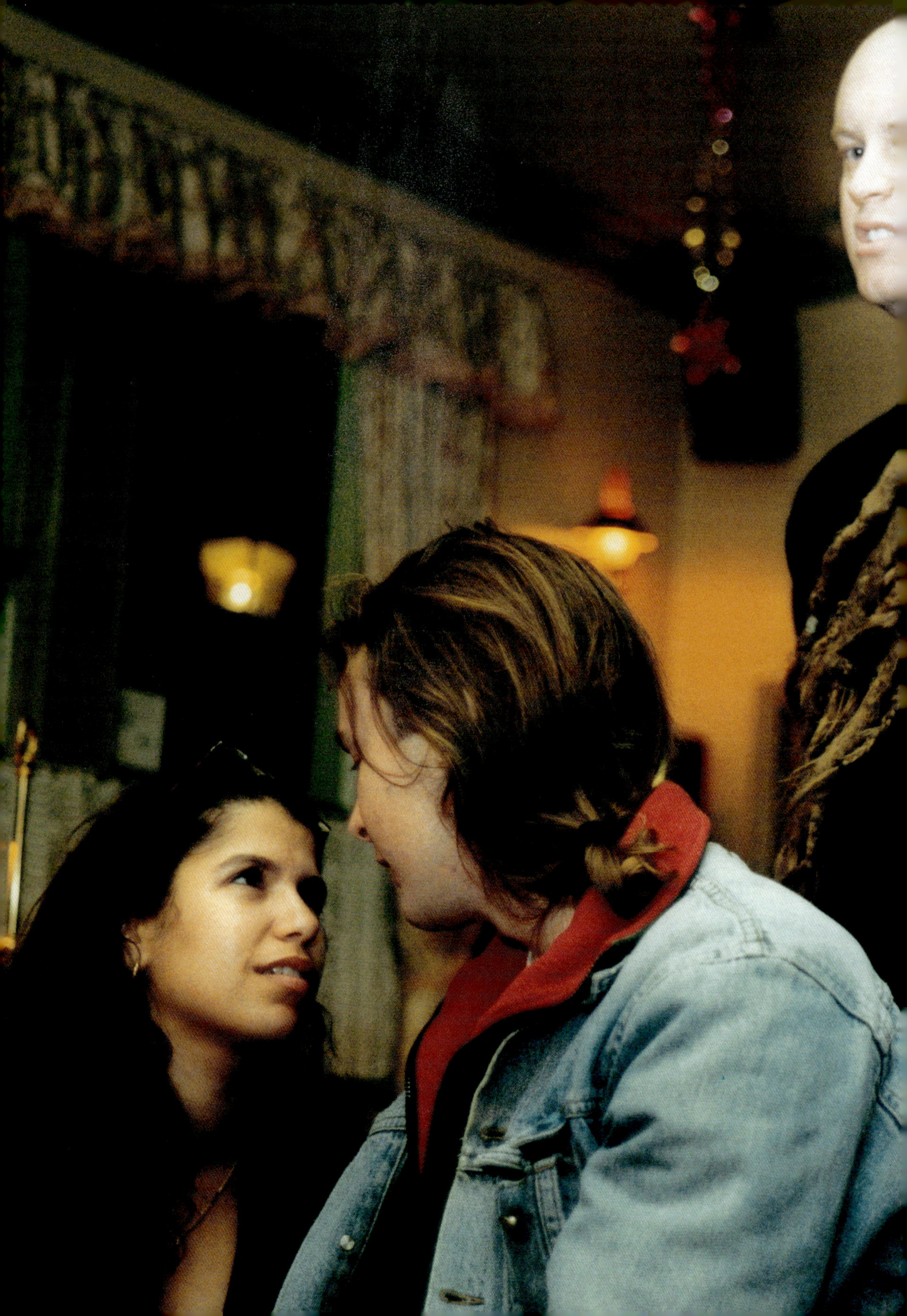

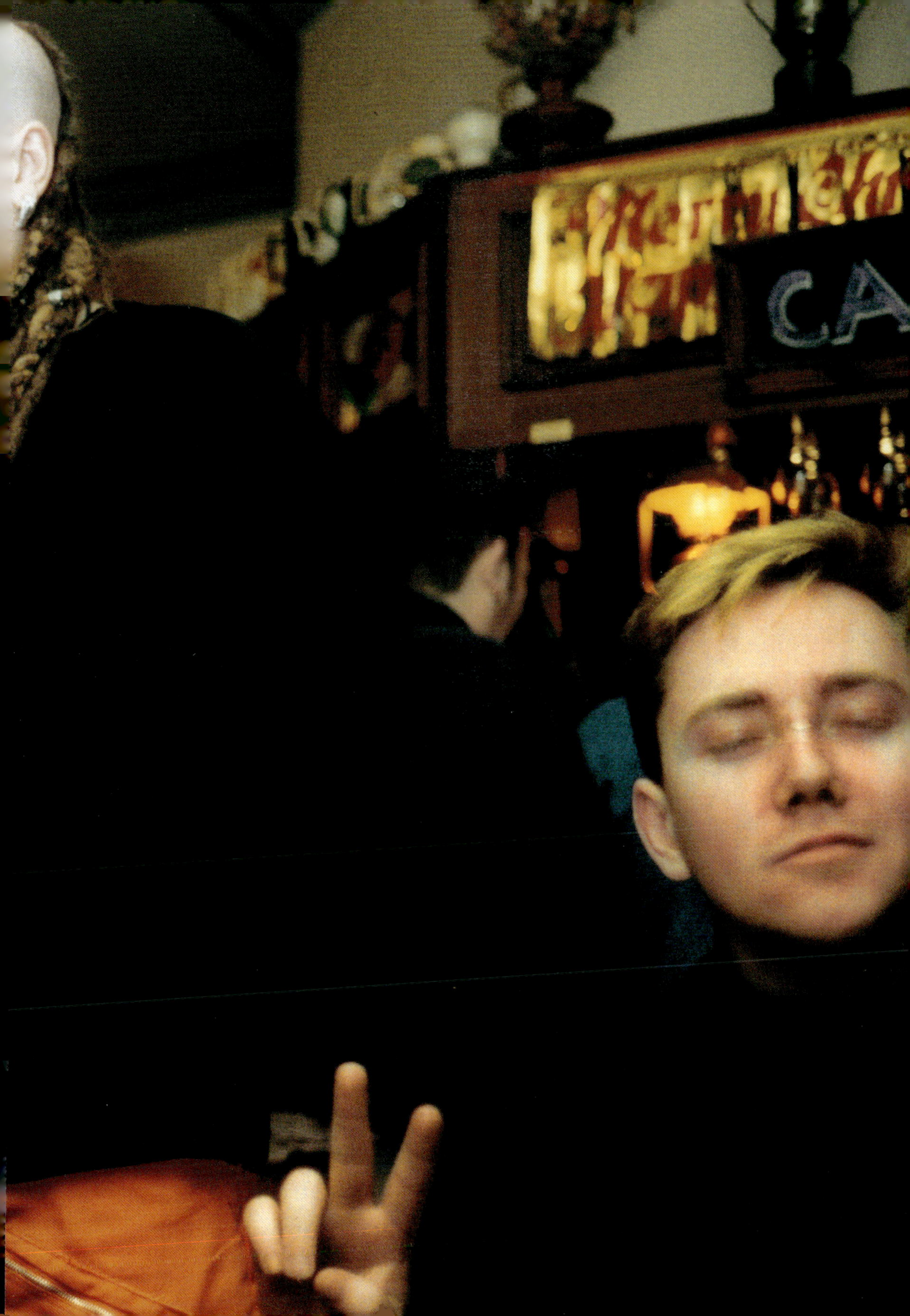
CA

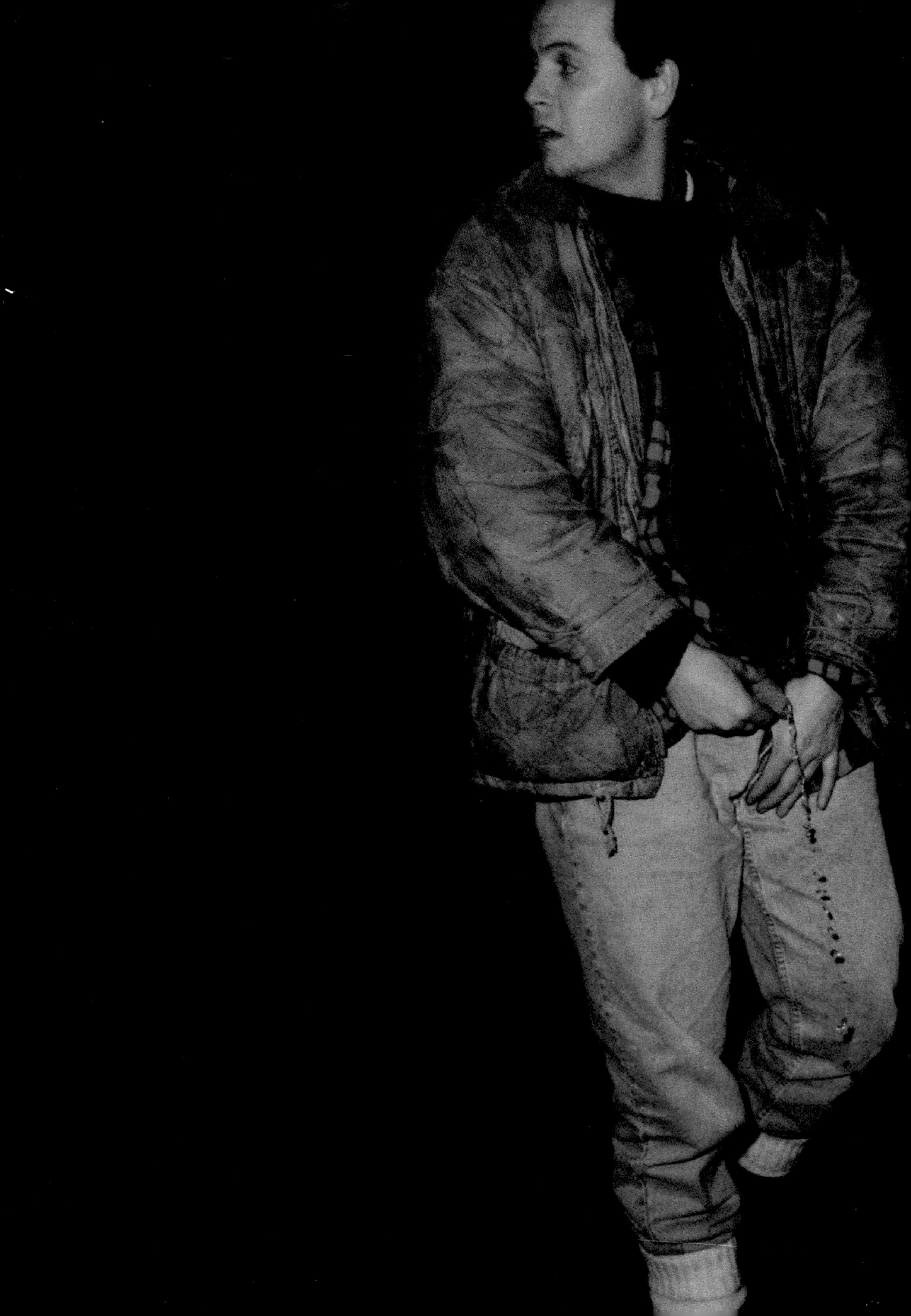

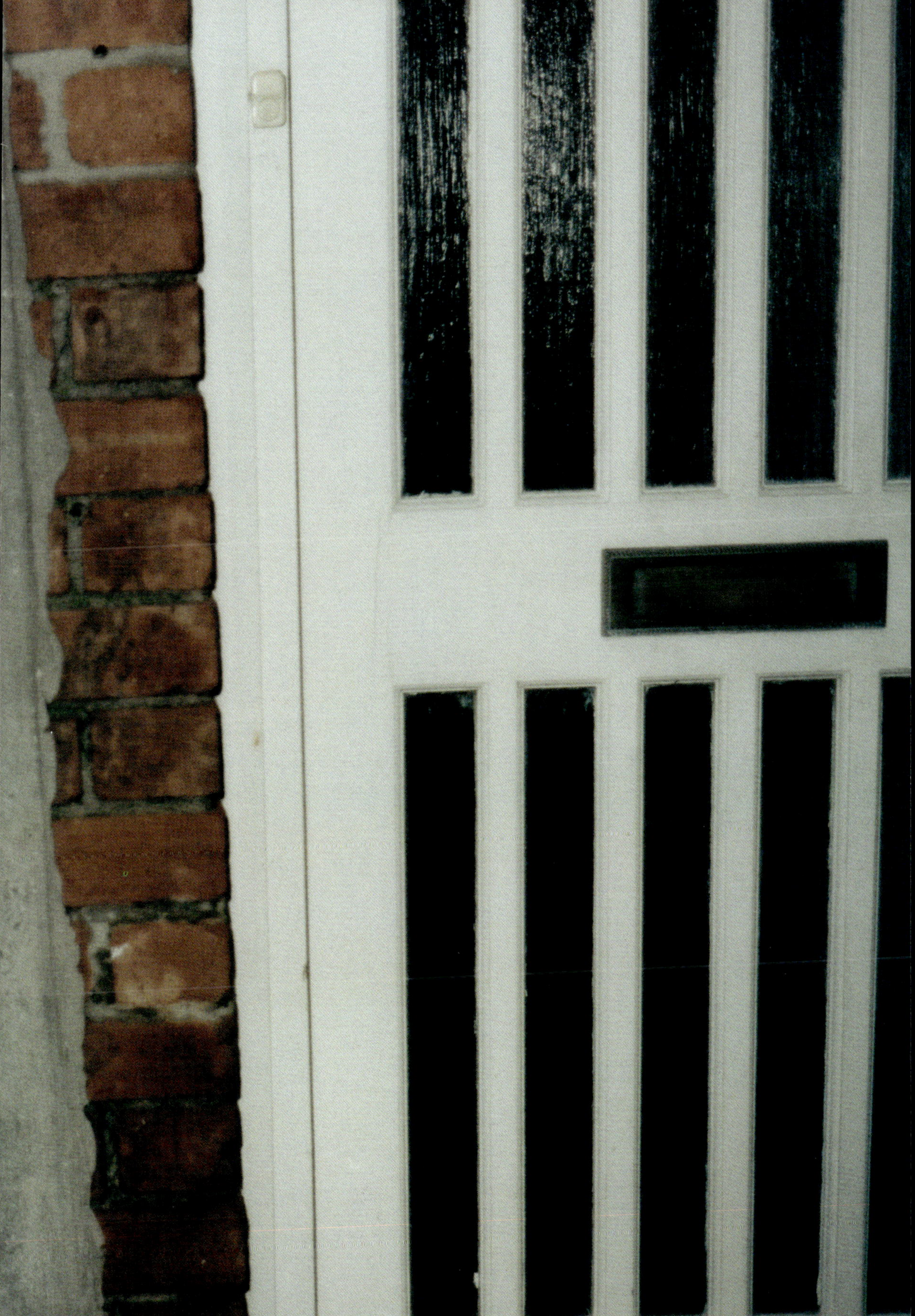

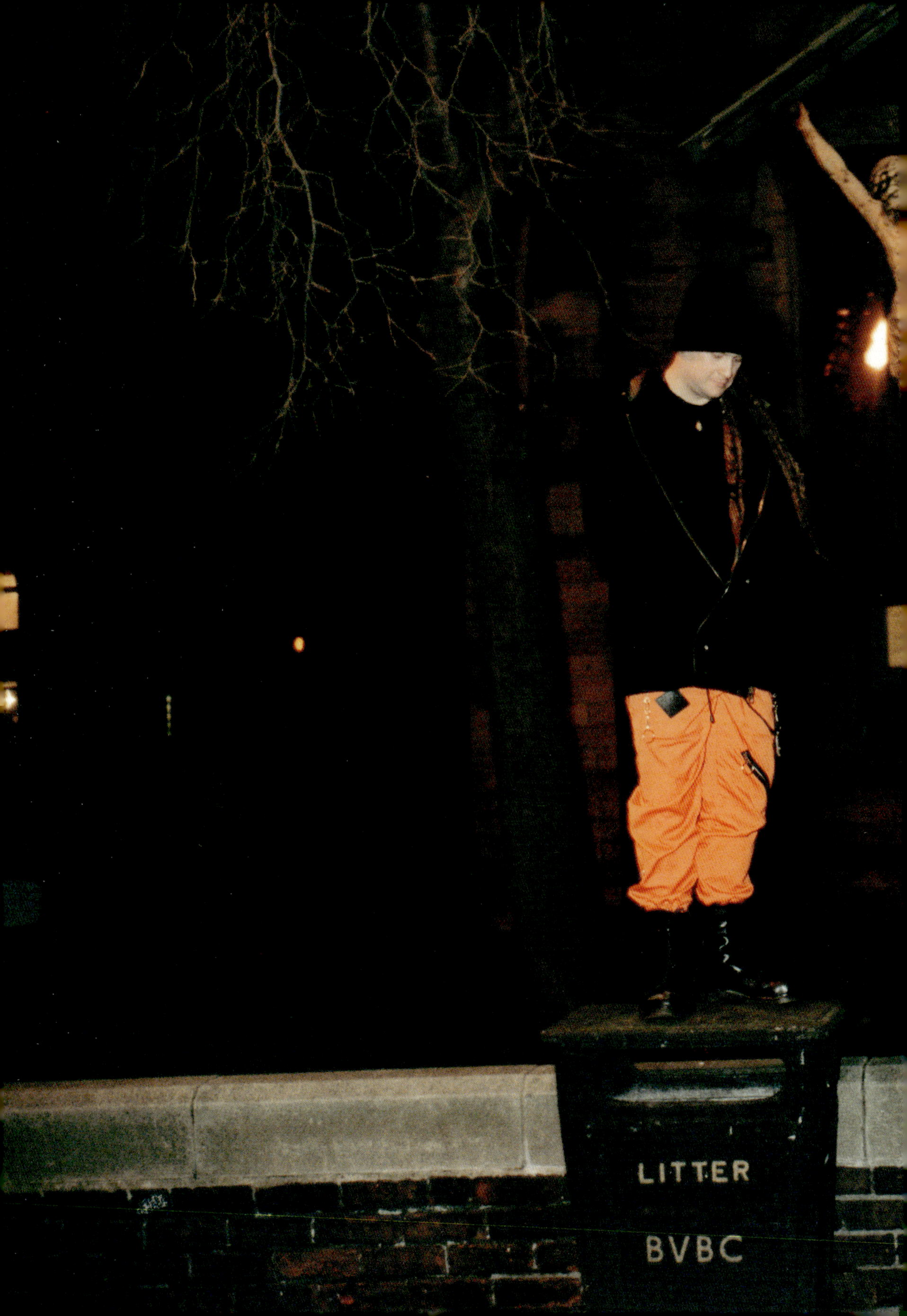
LITTER
BVBC

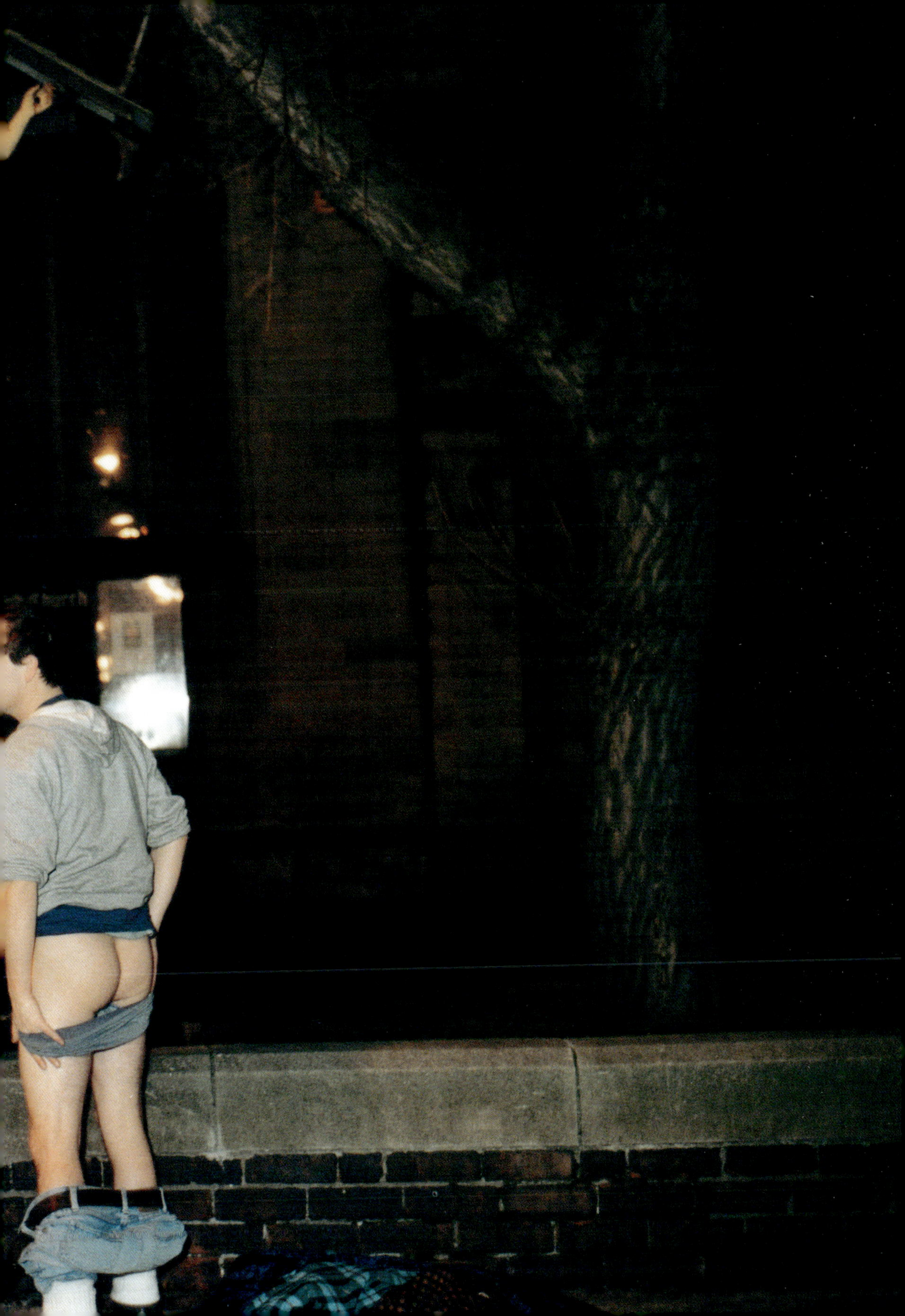

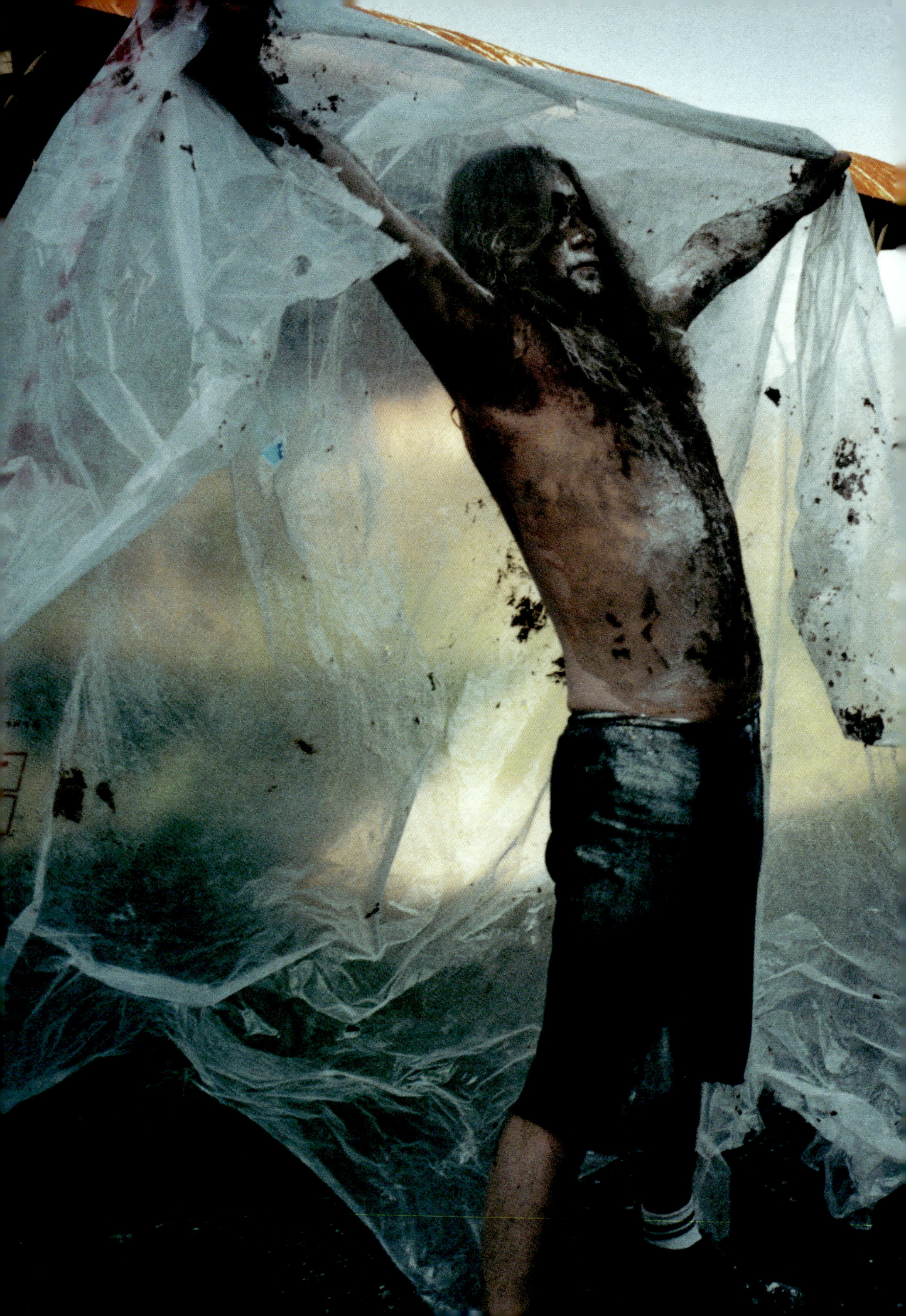

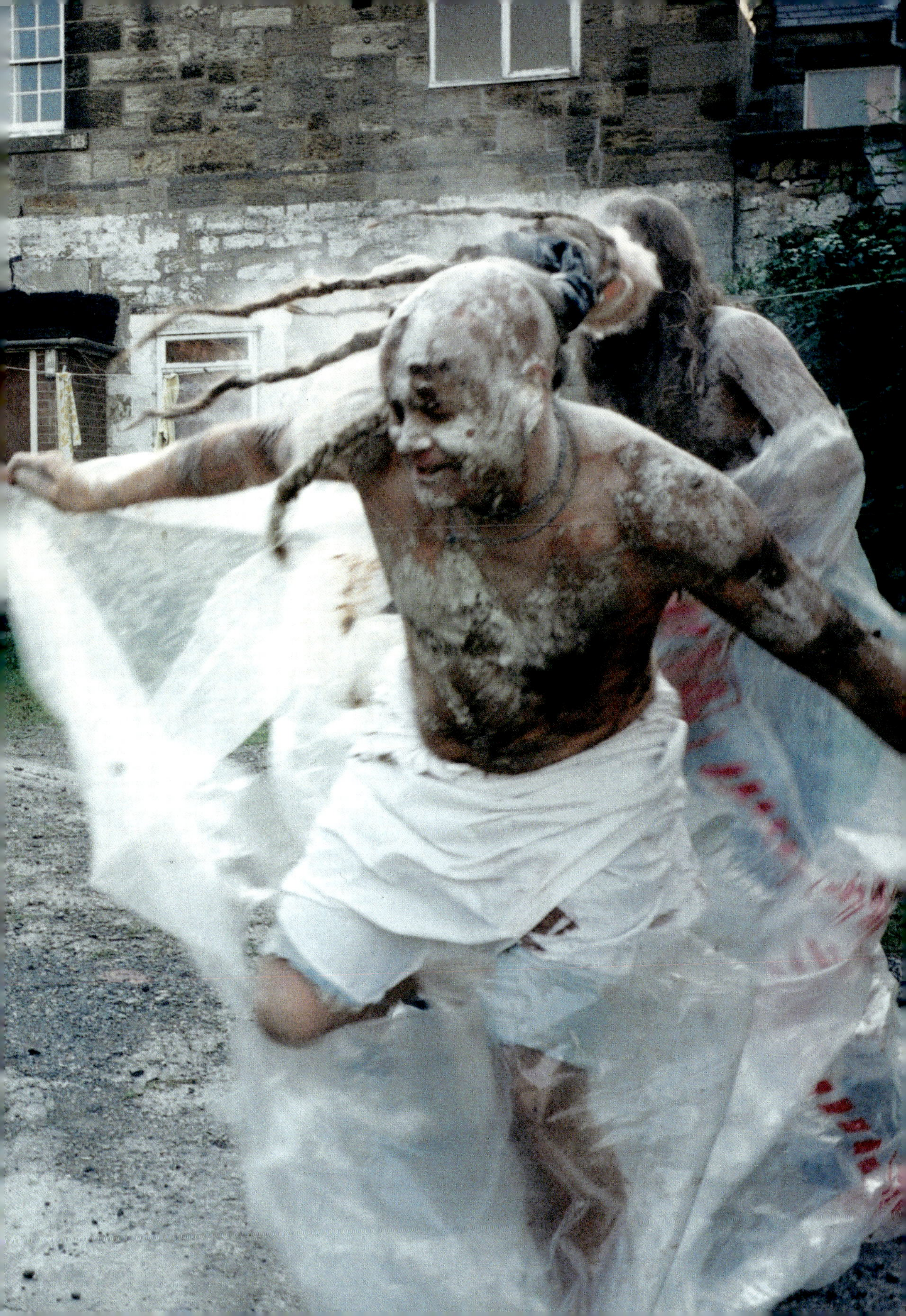

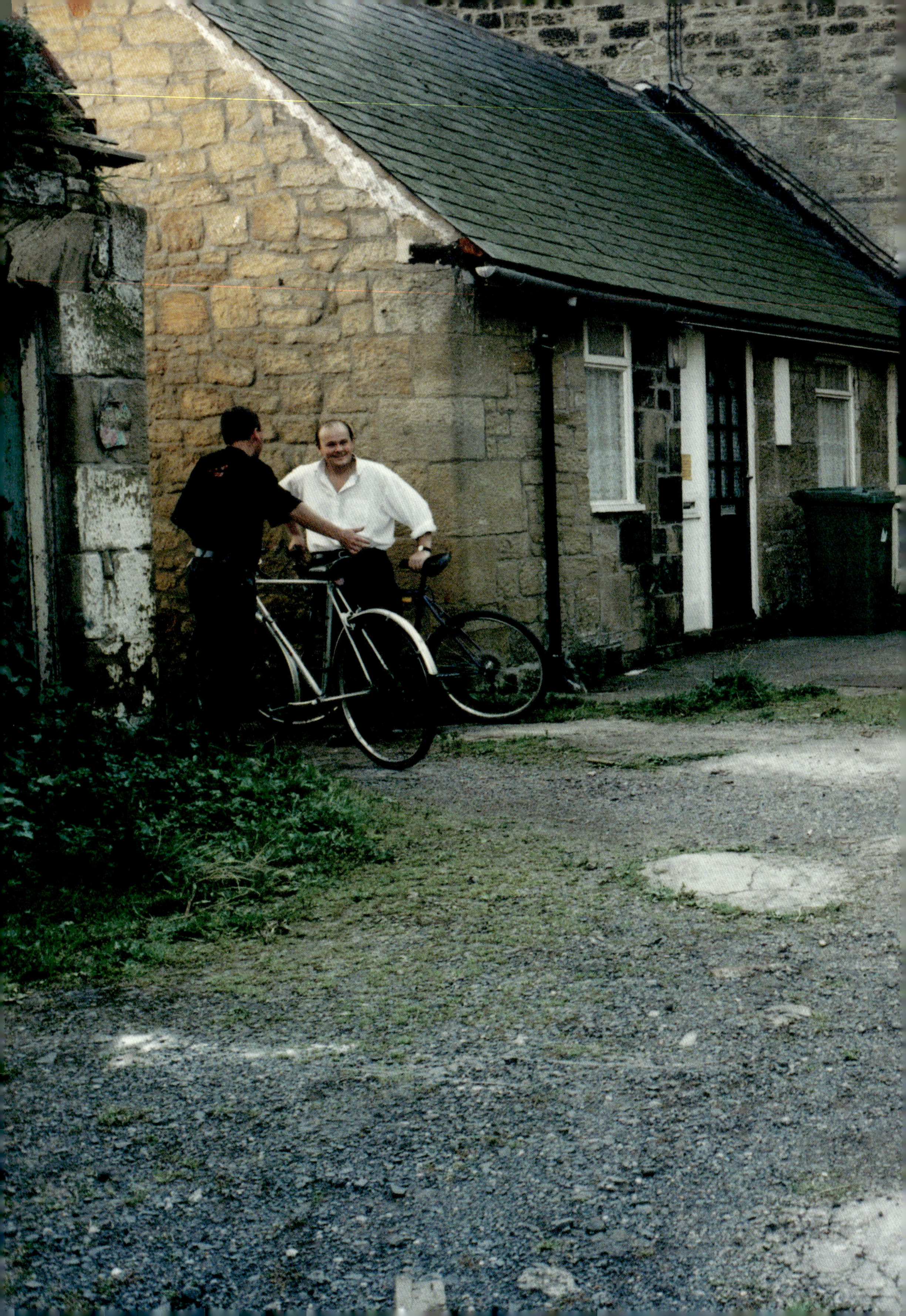

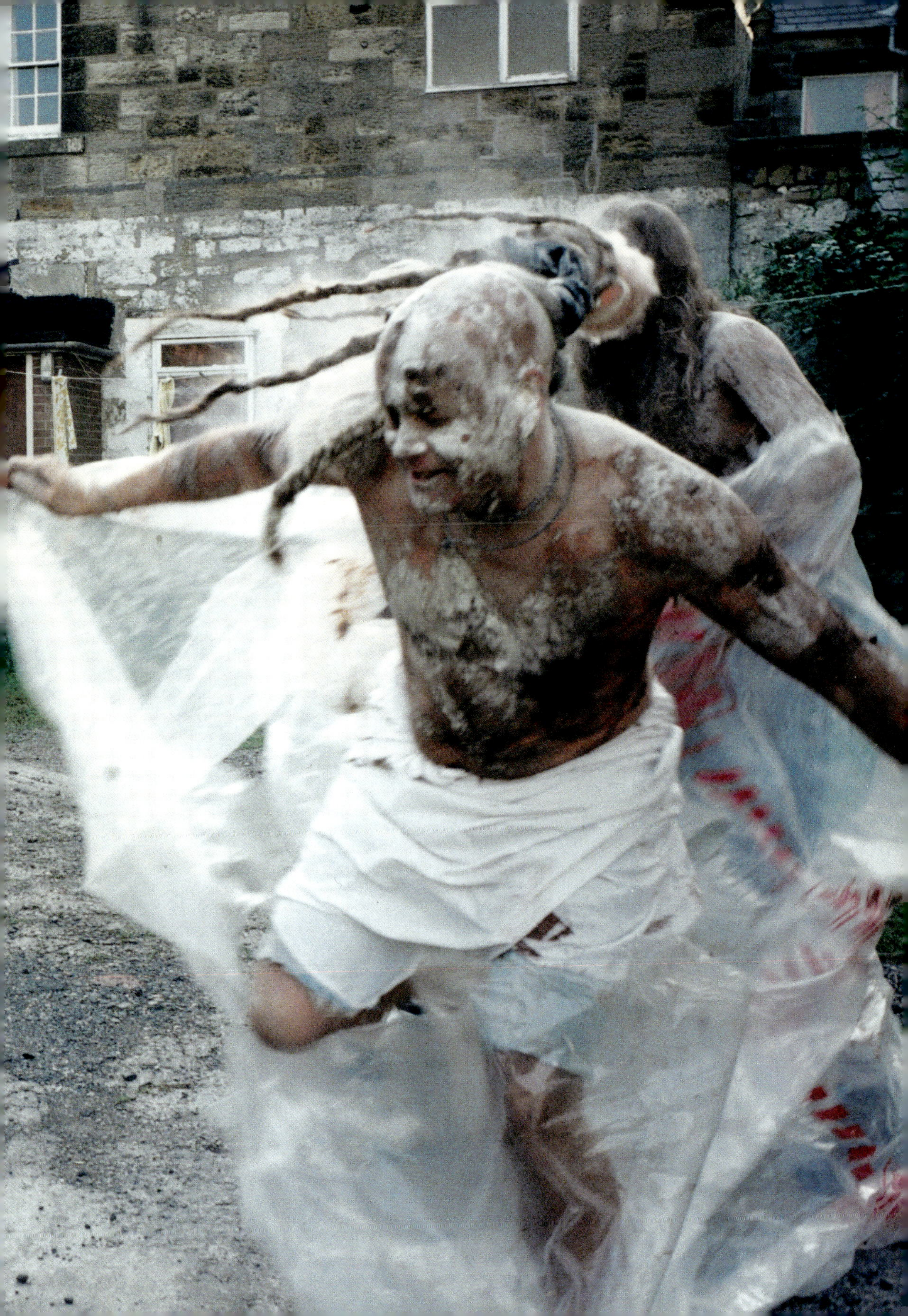

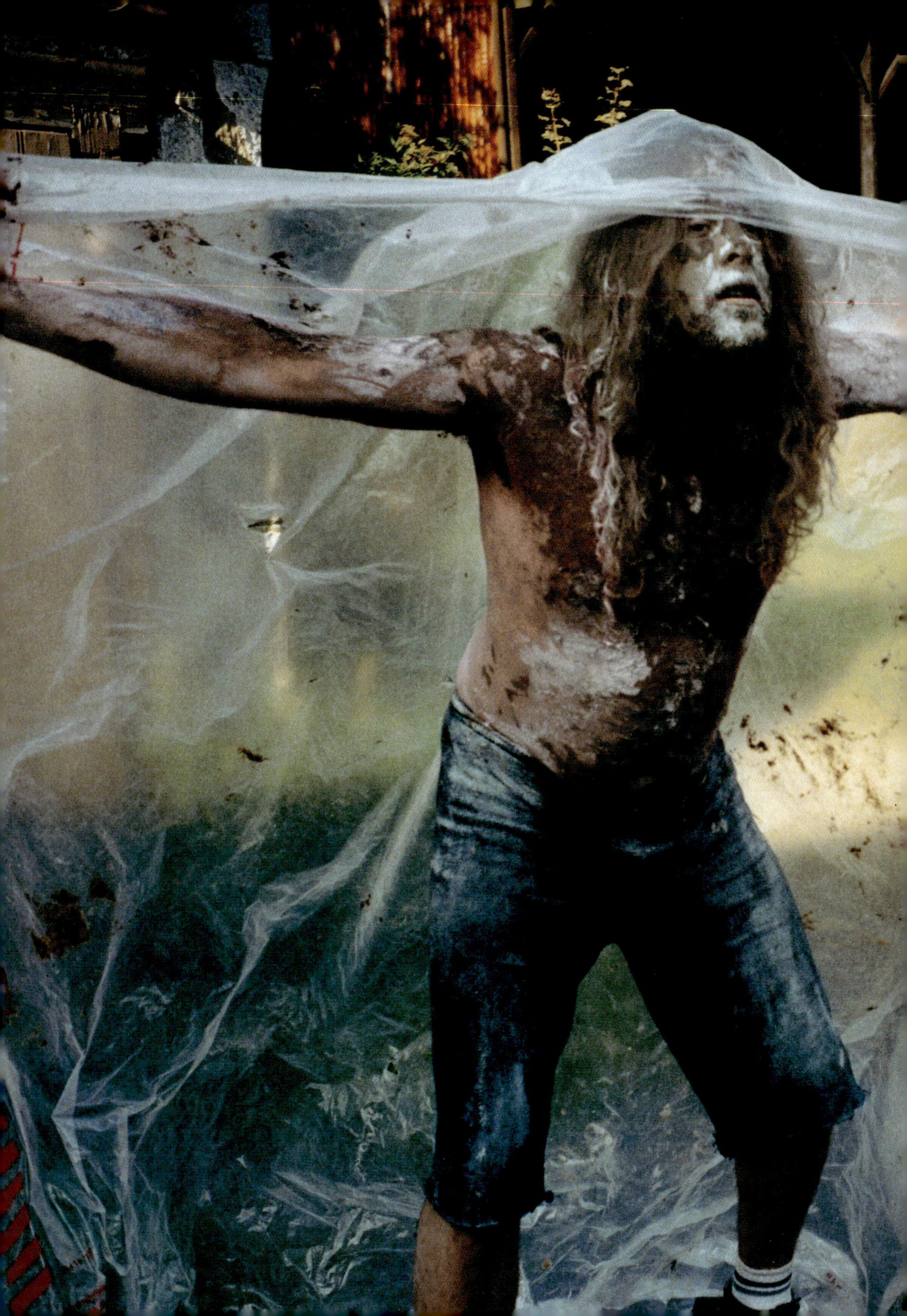

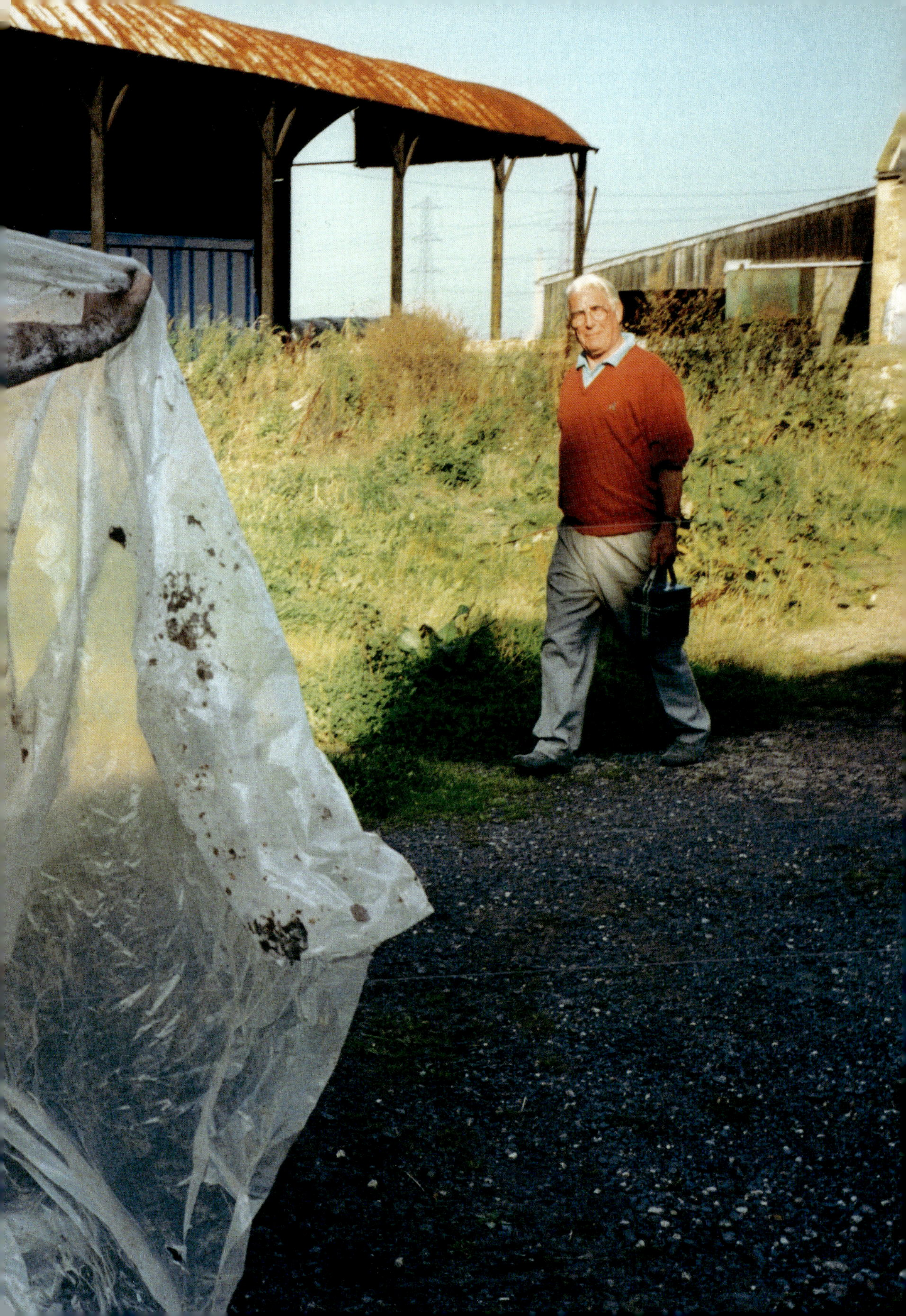

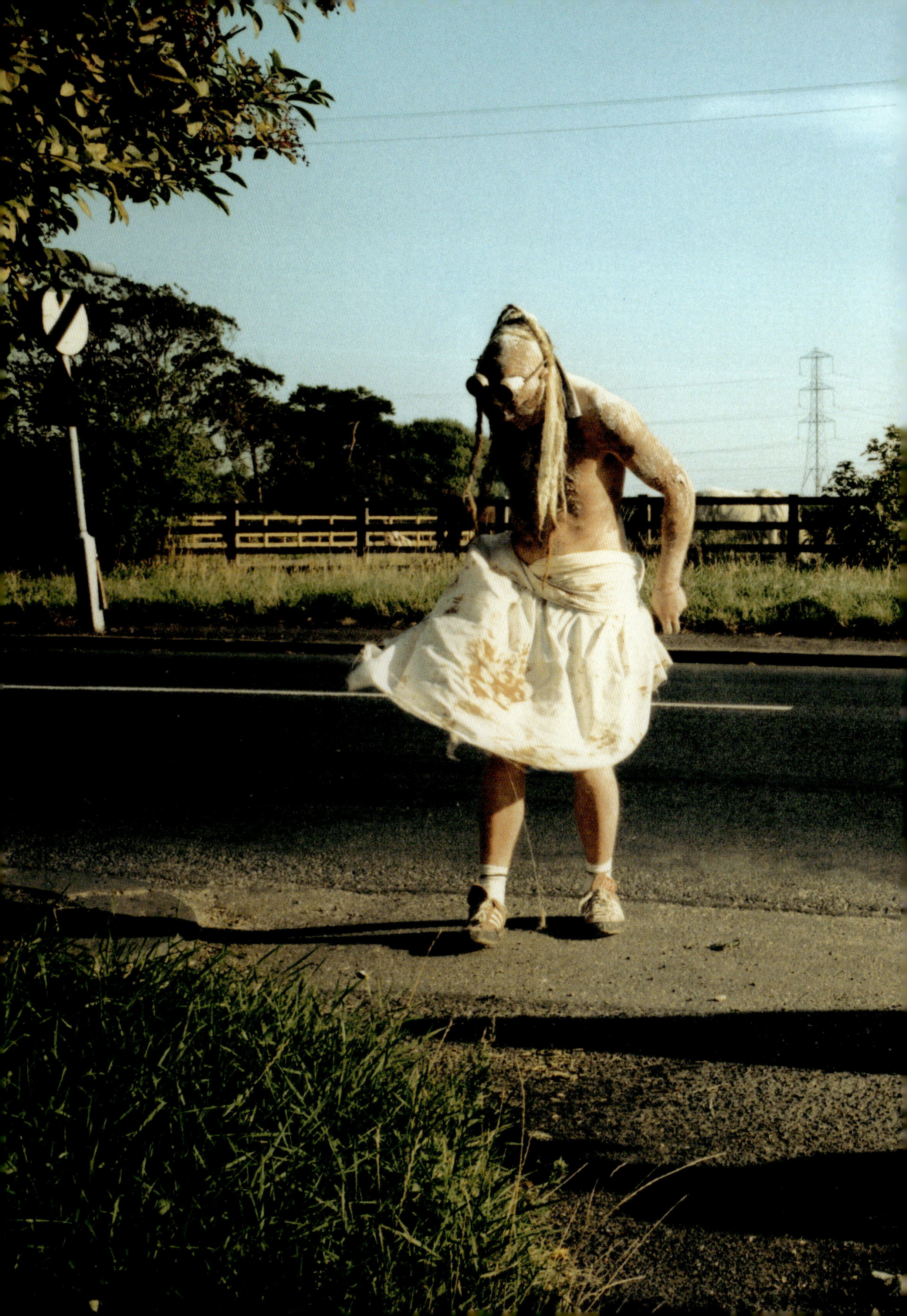

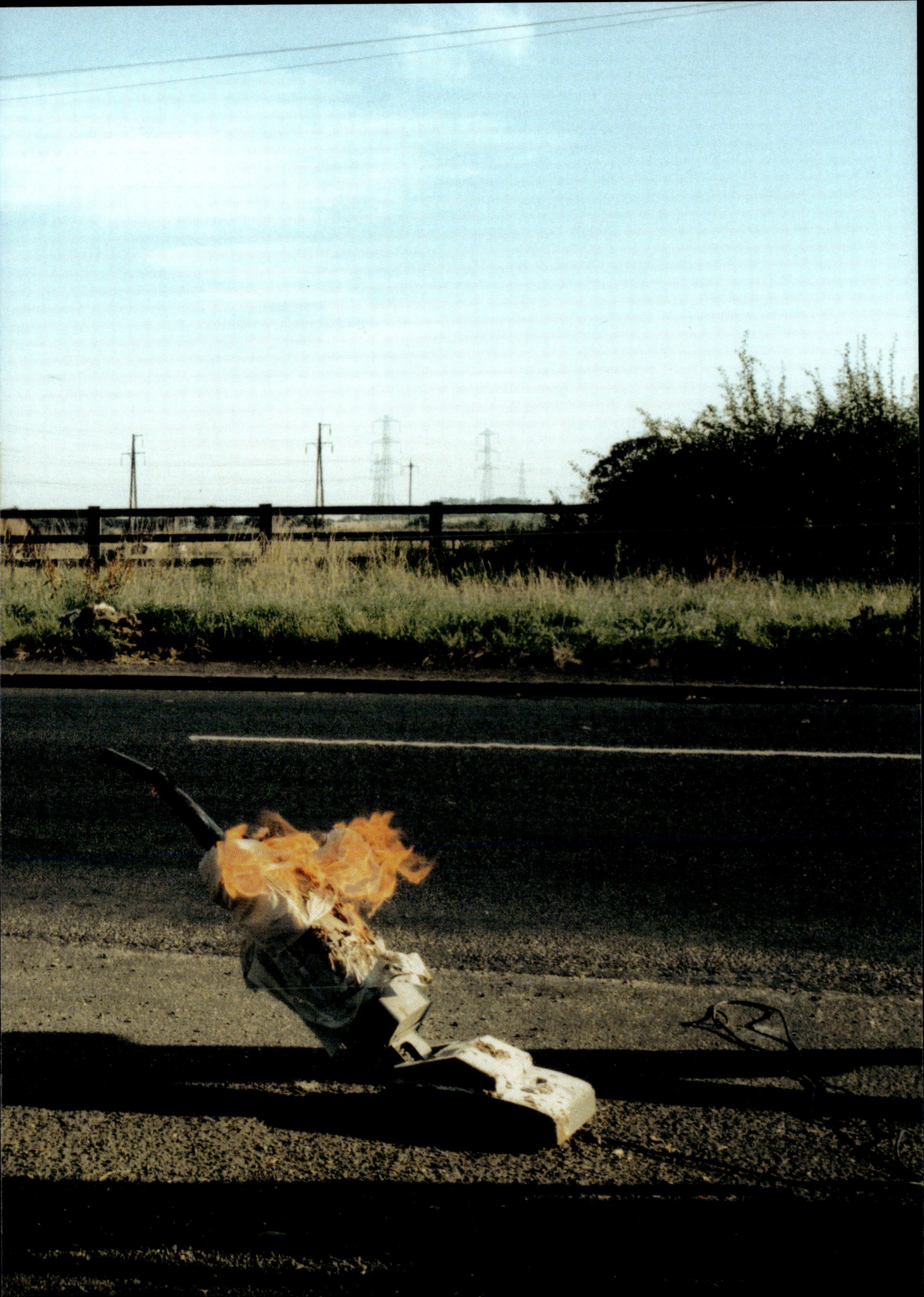

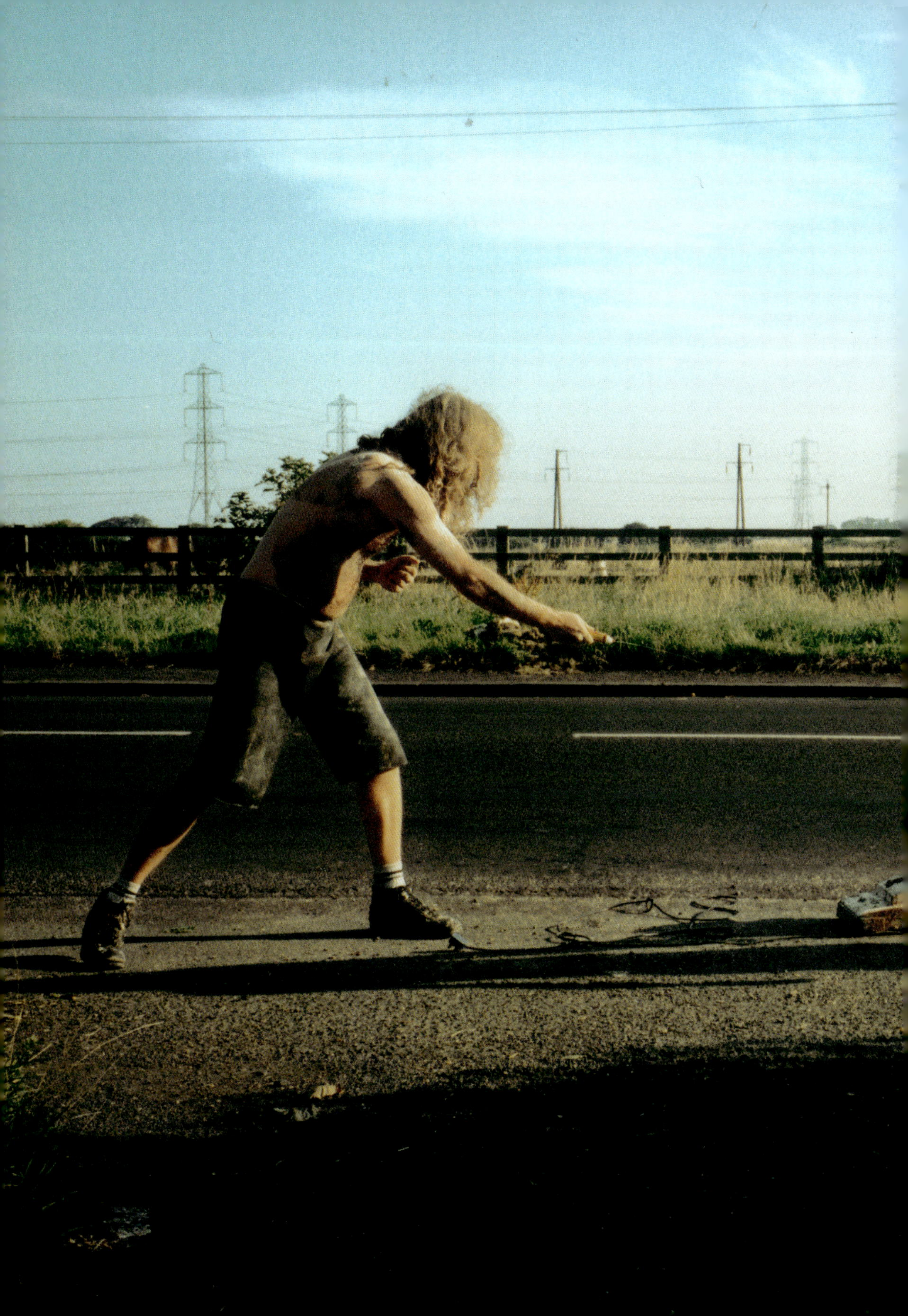

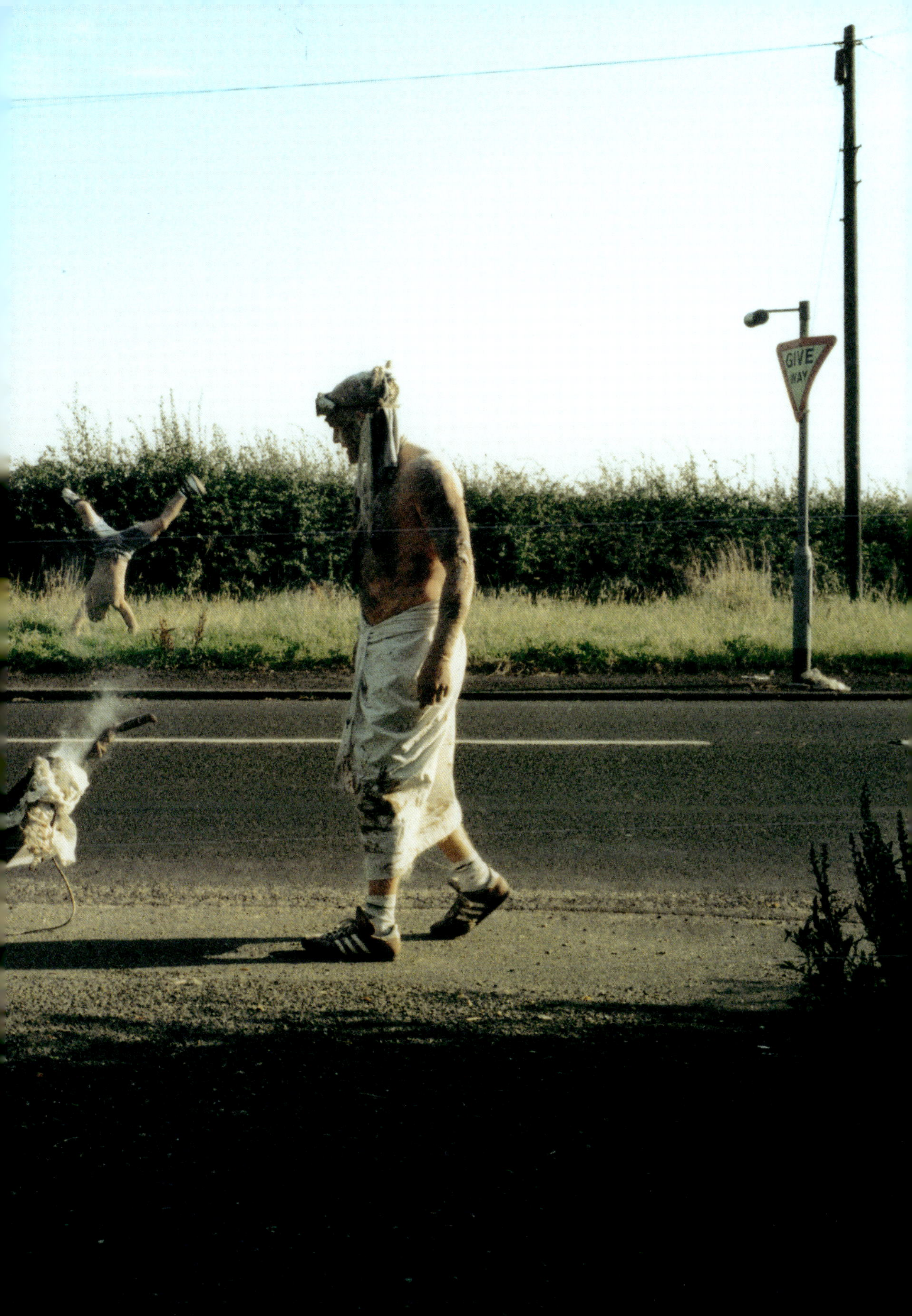
GIVE
WAY

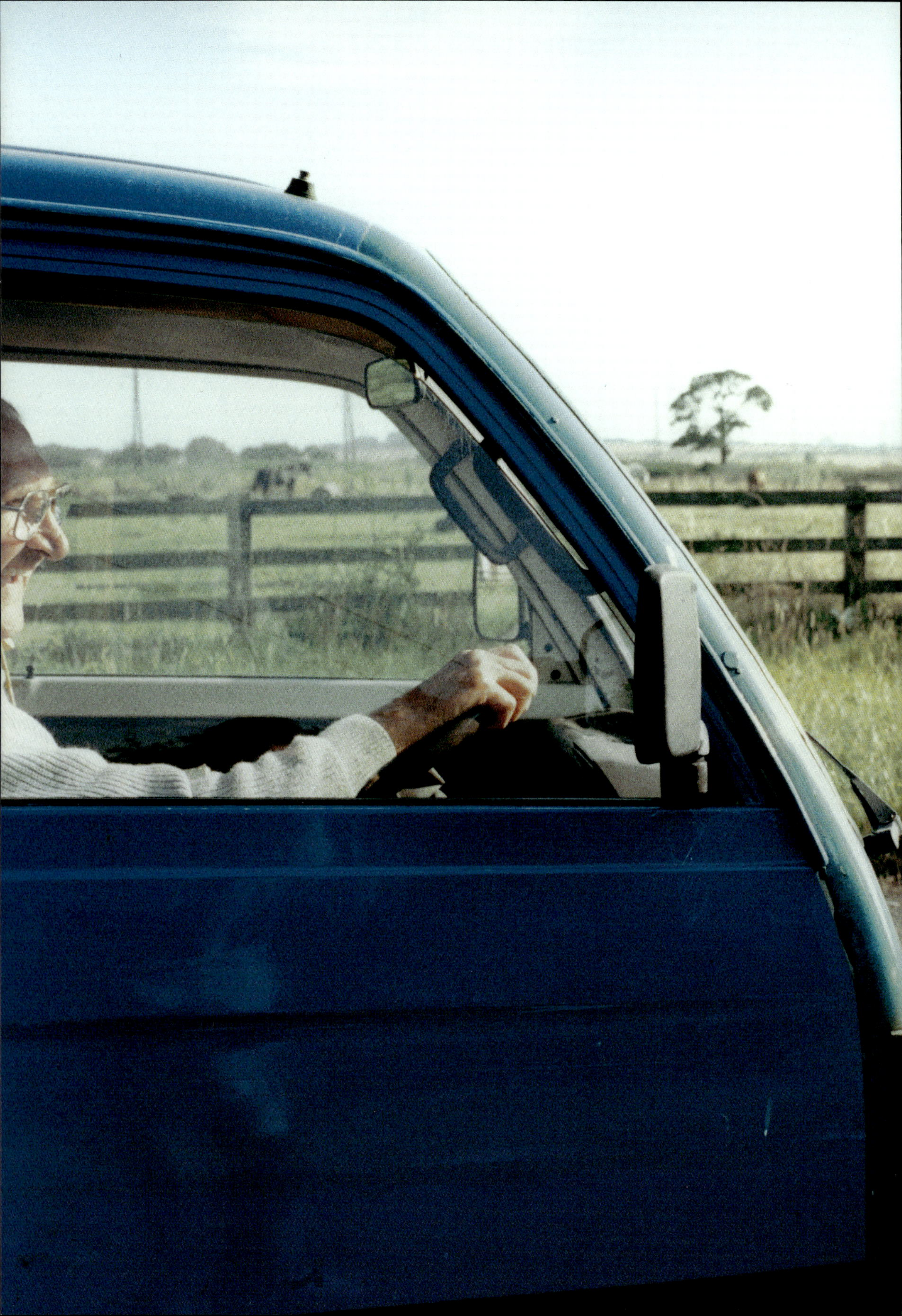

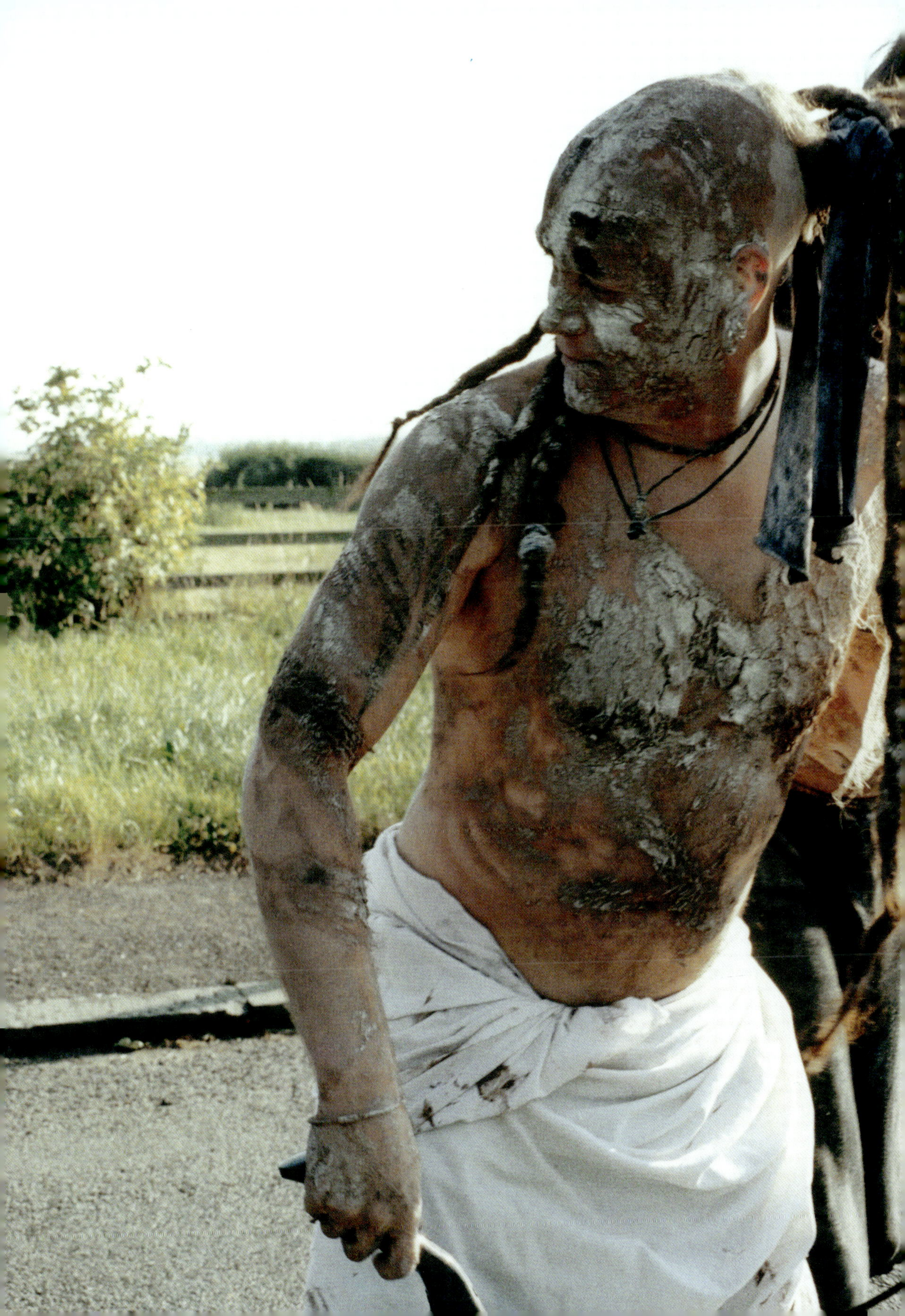

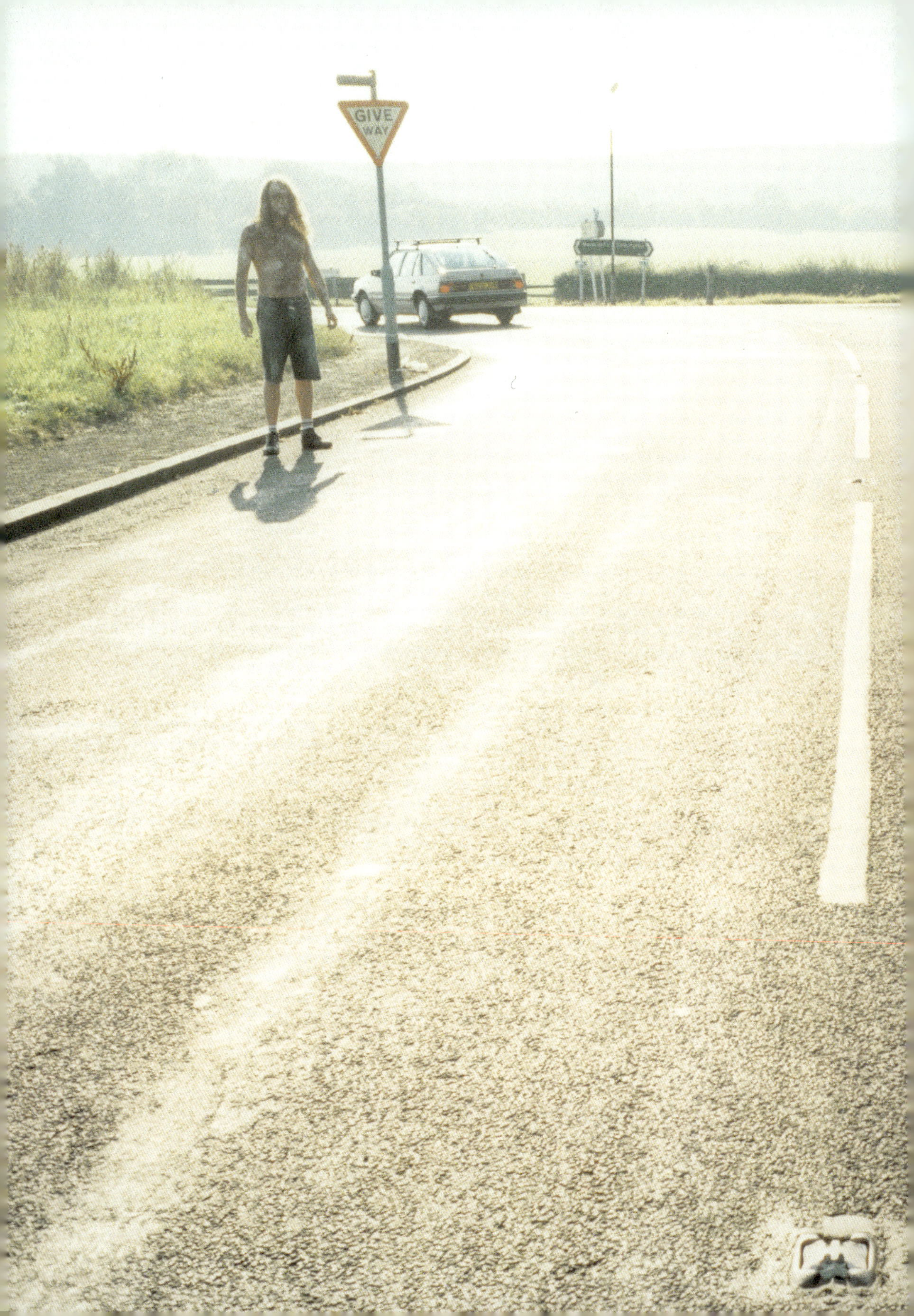
GIVE
WAY

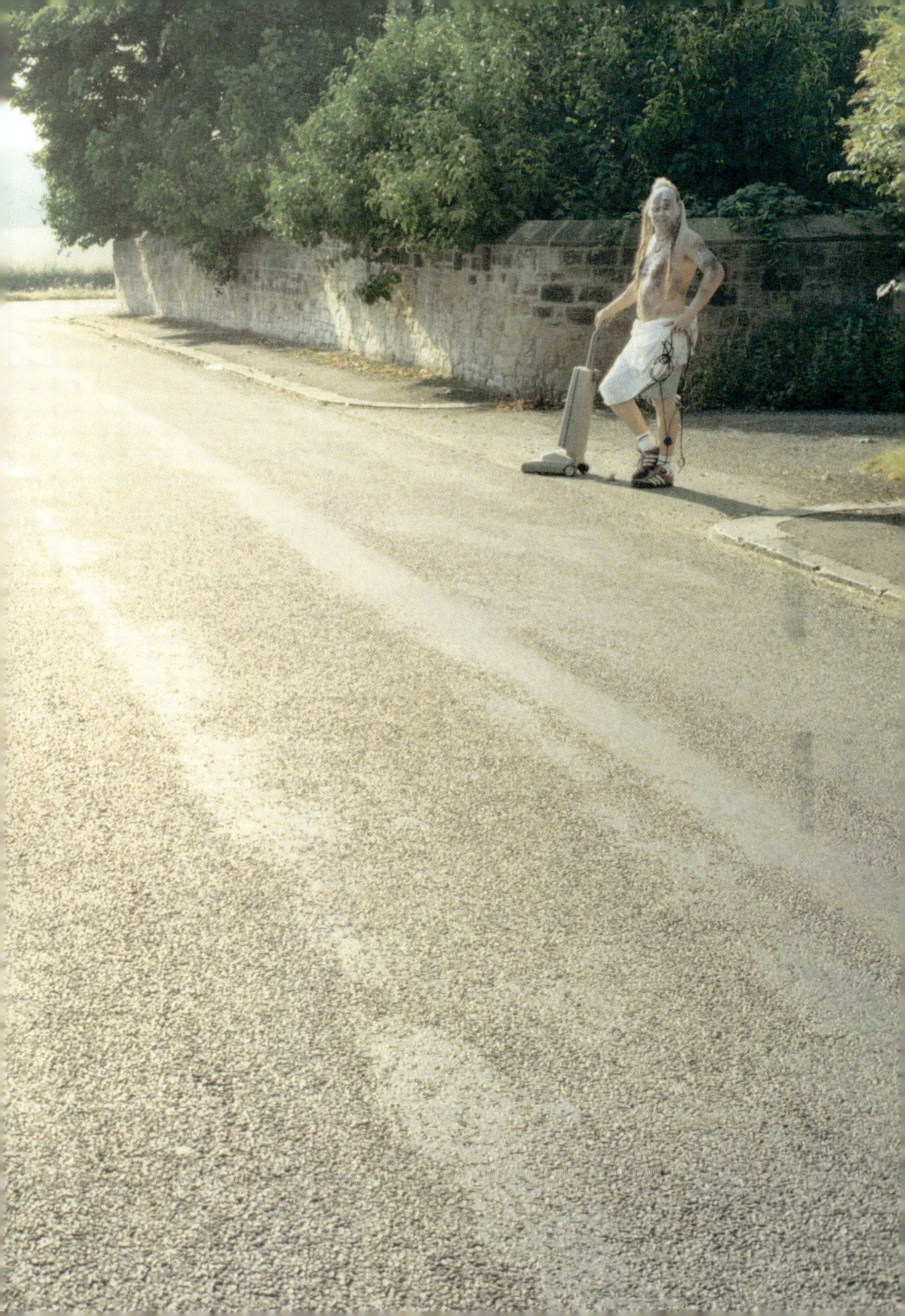

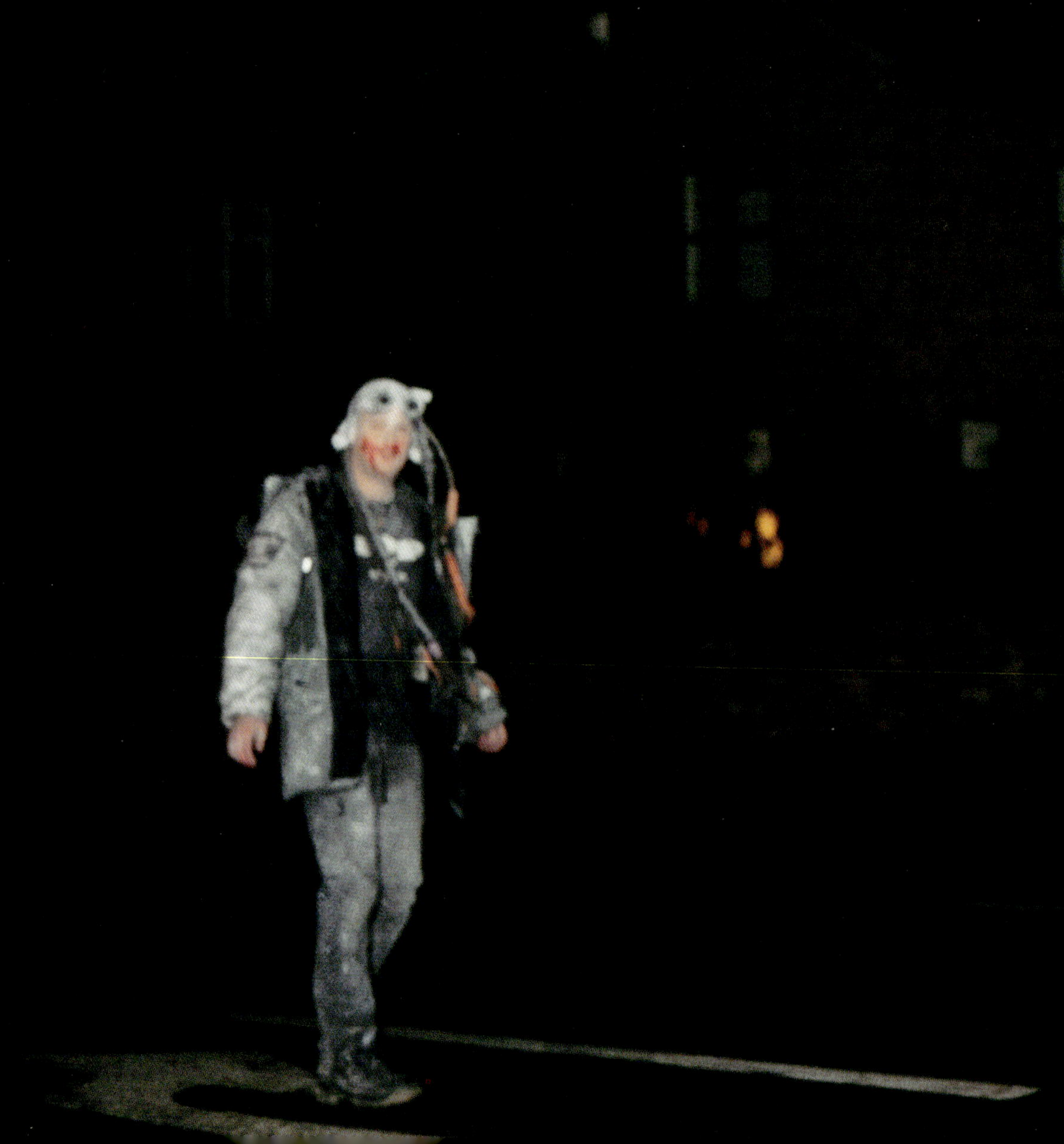

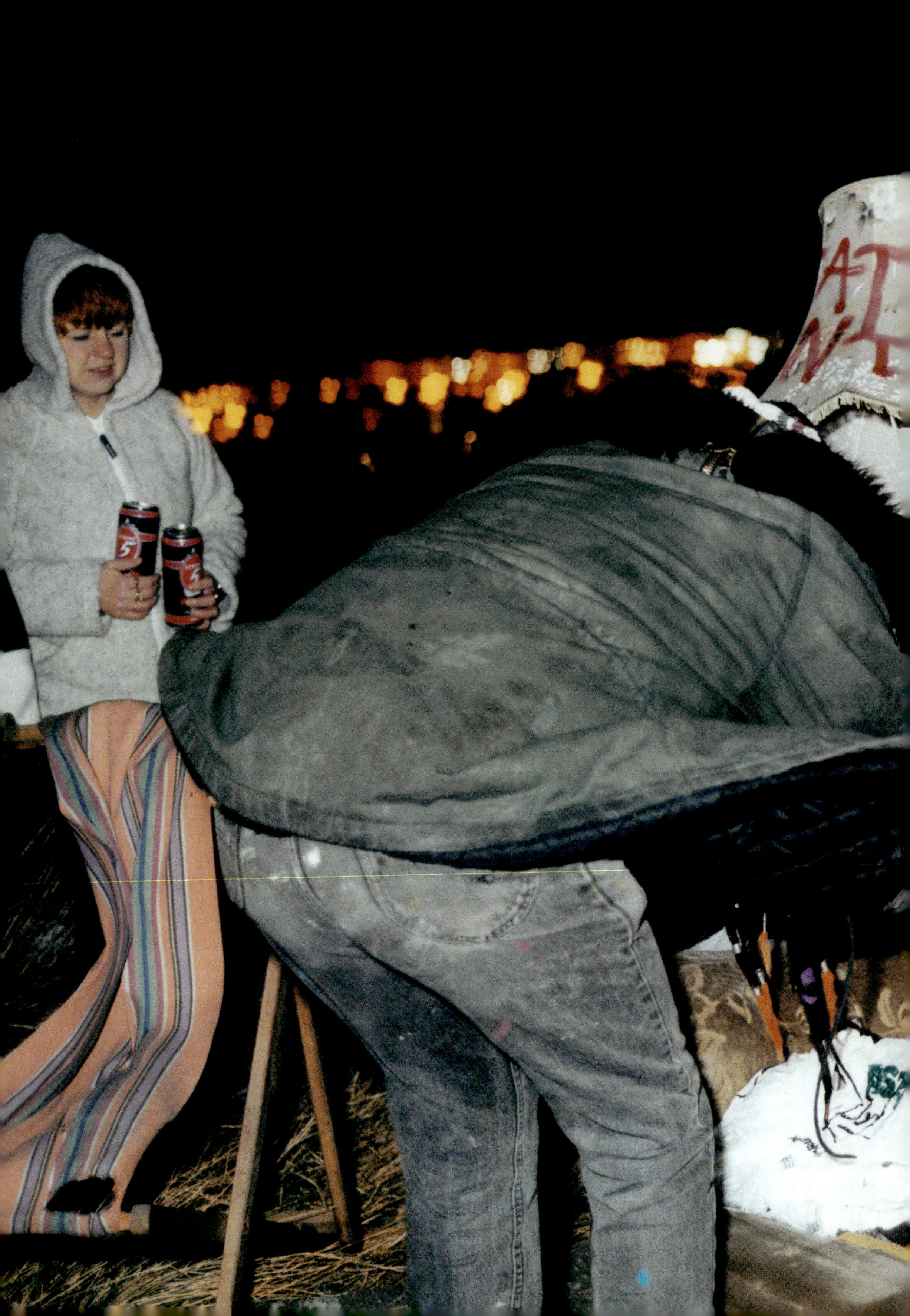

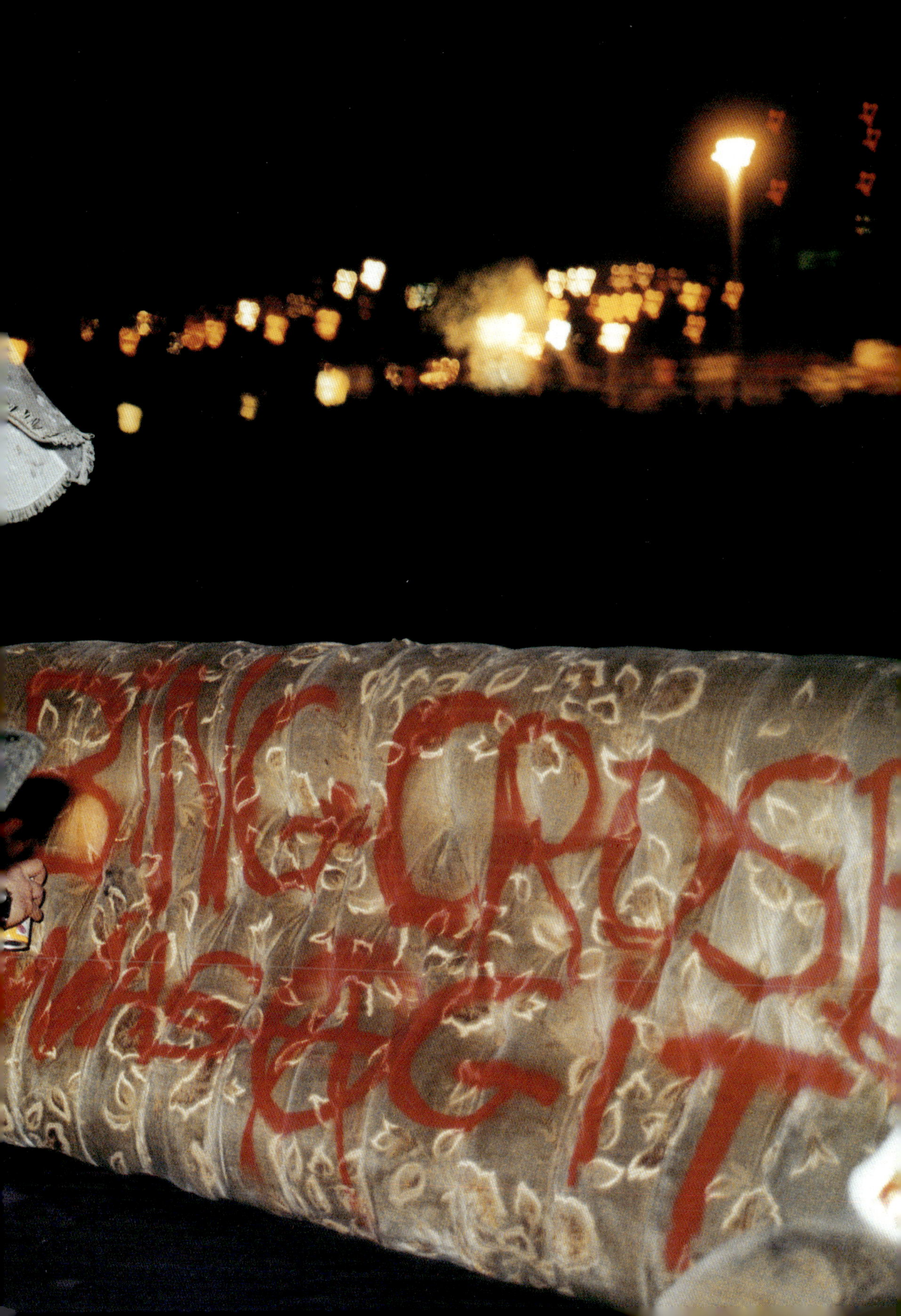

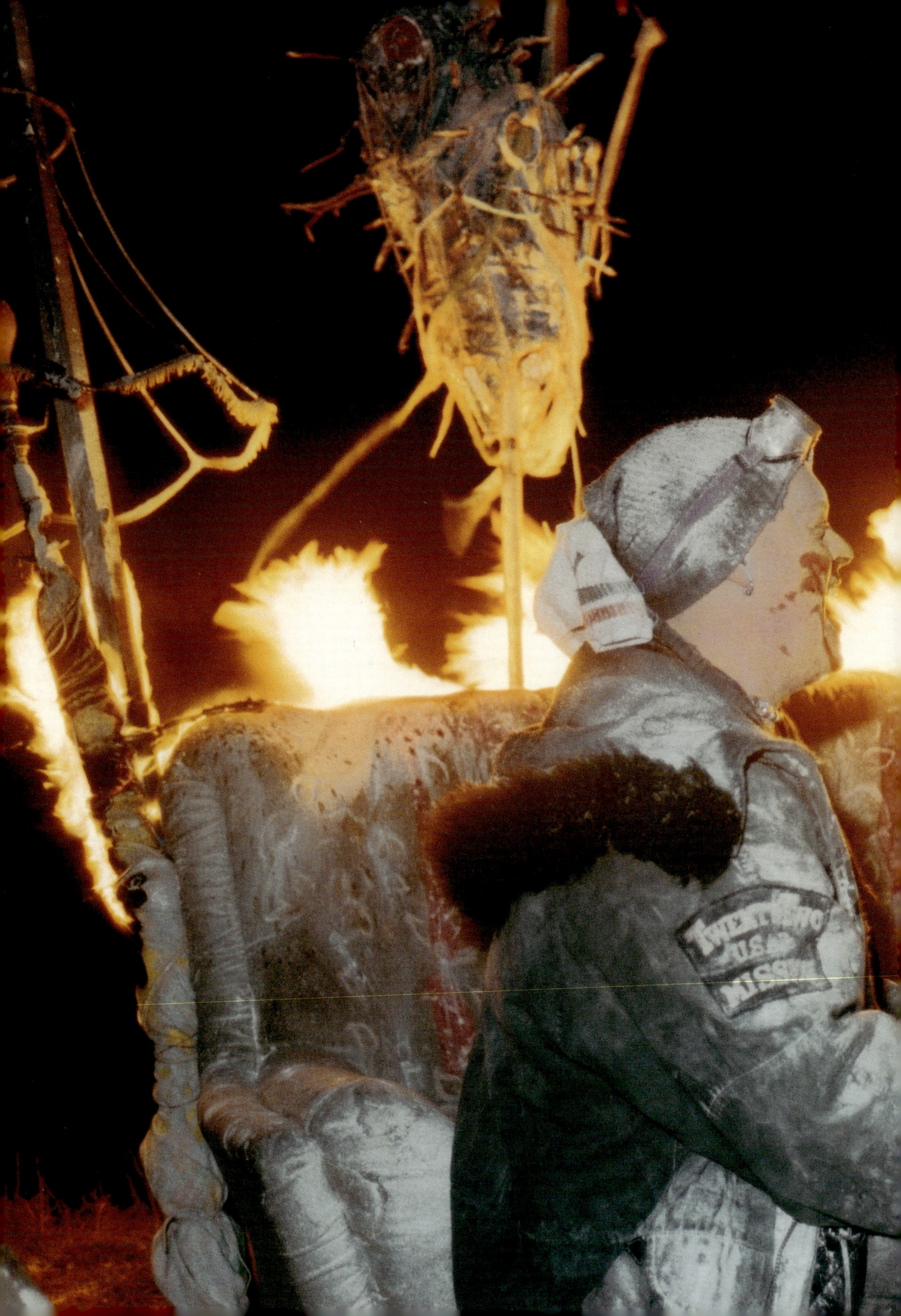

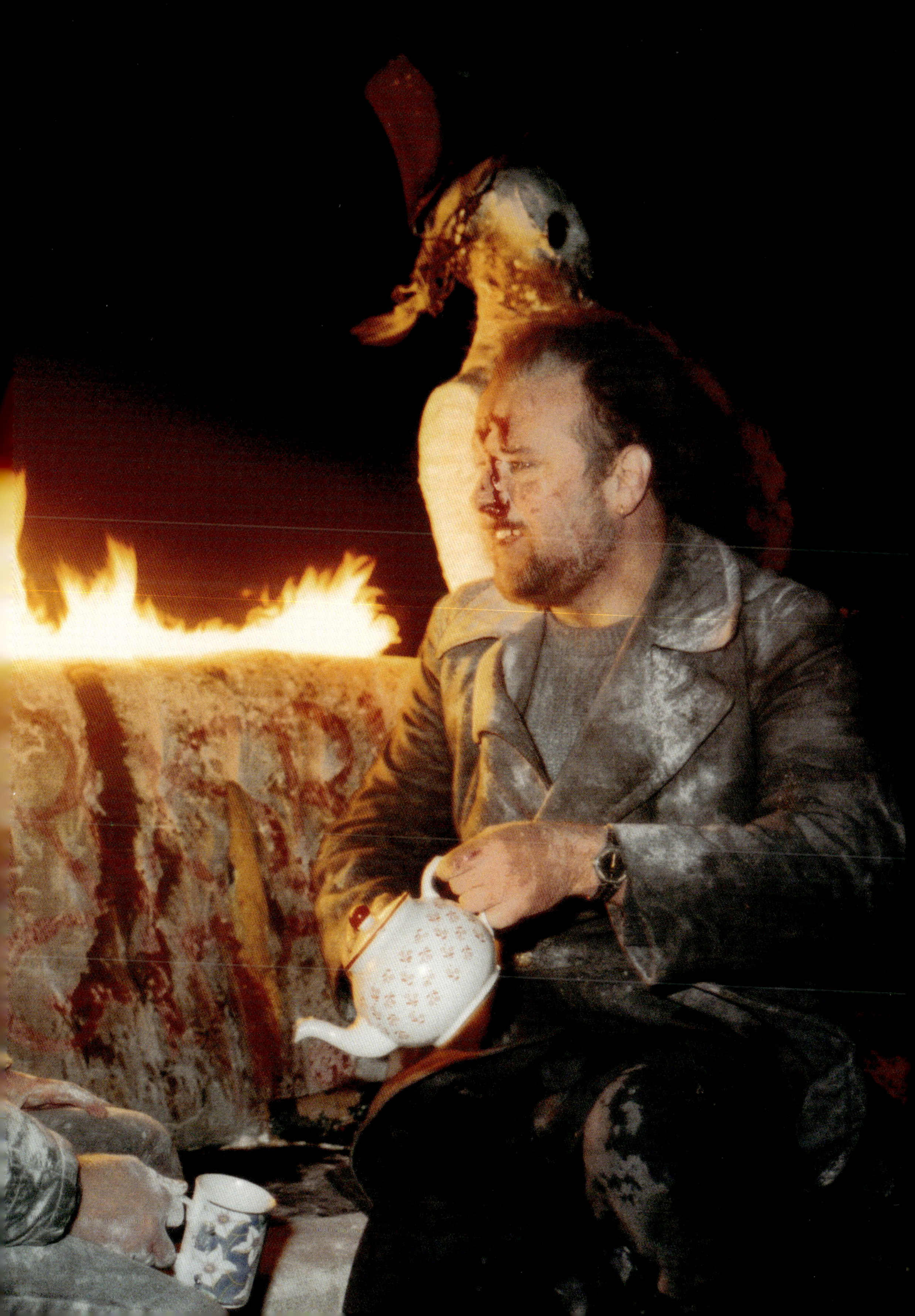

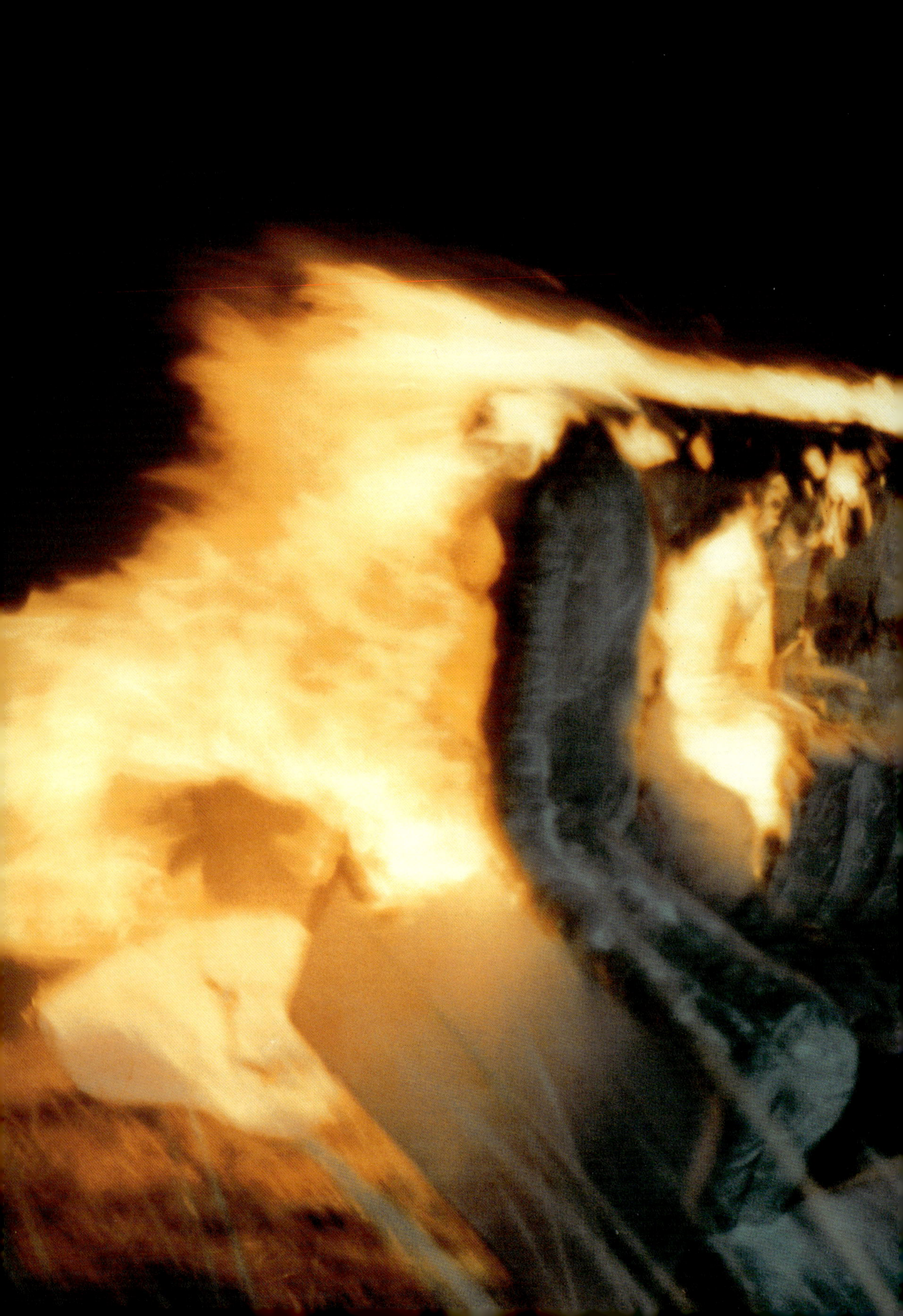

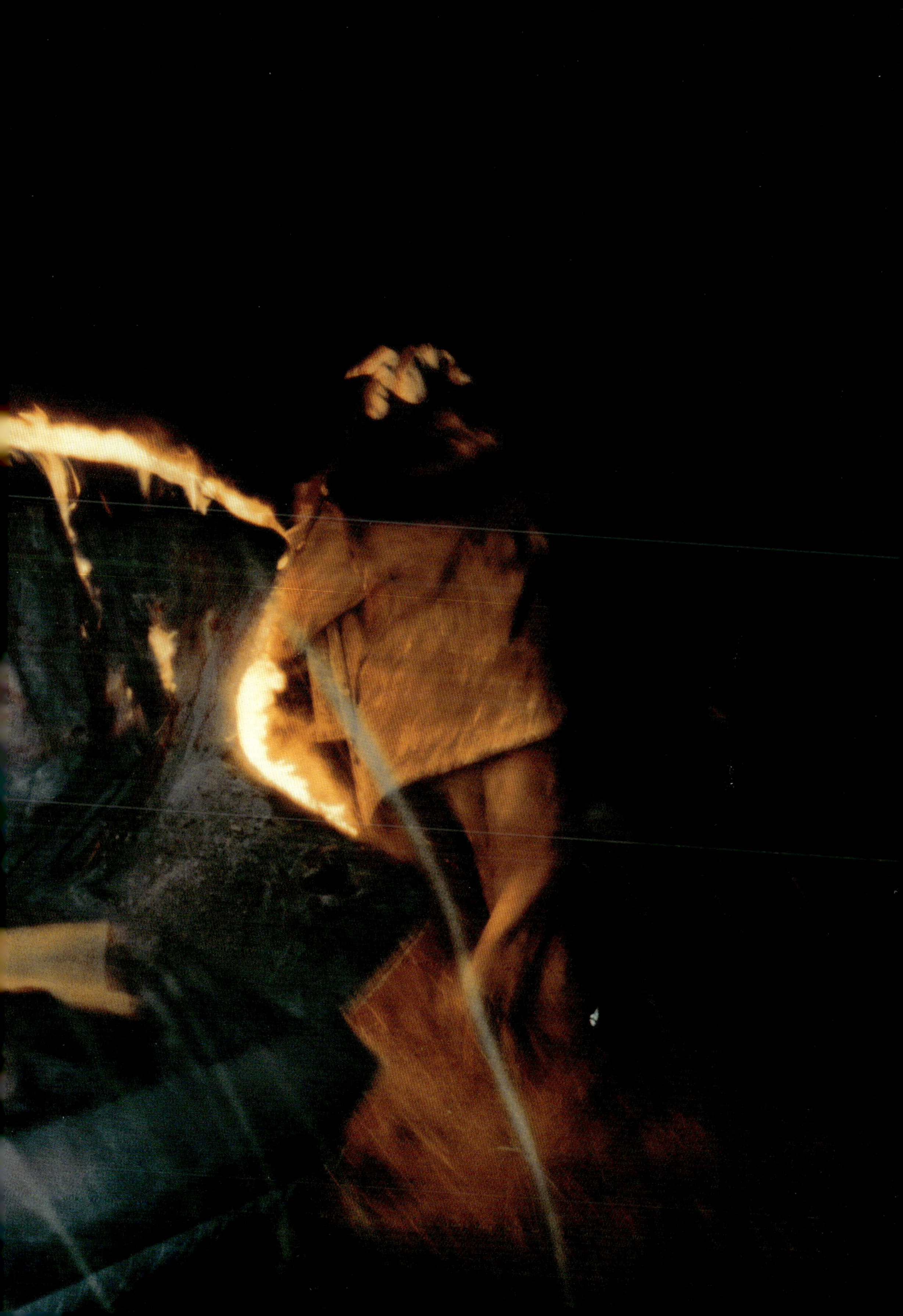

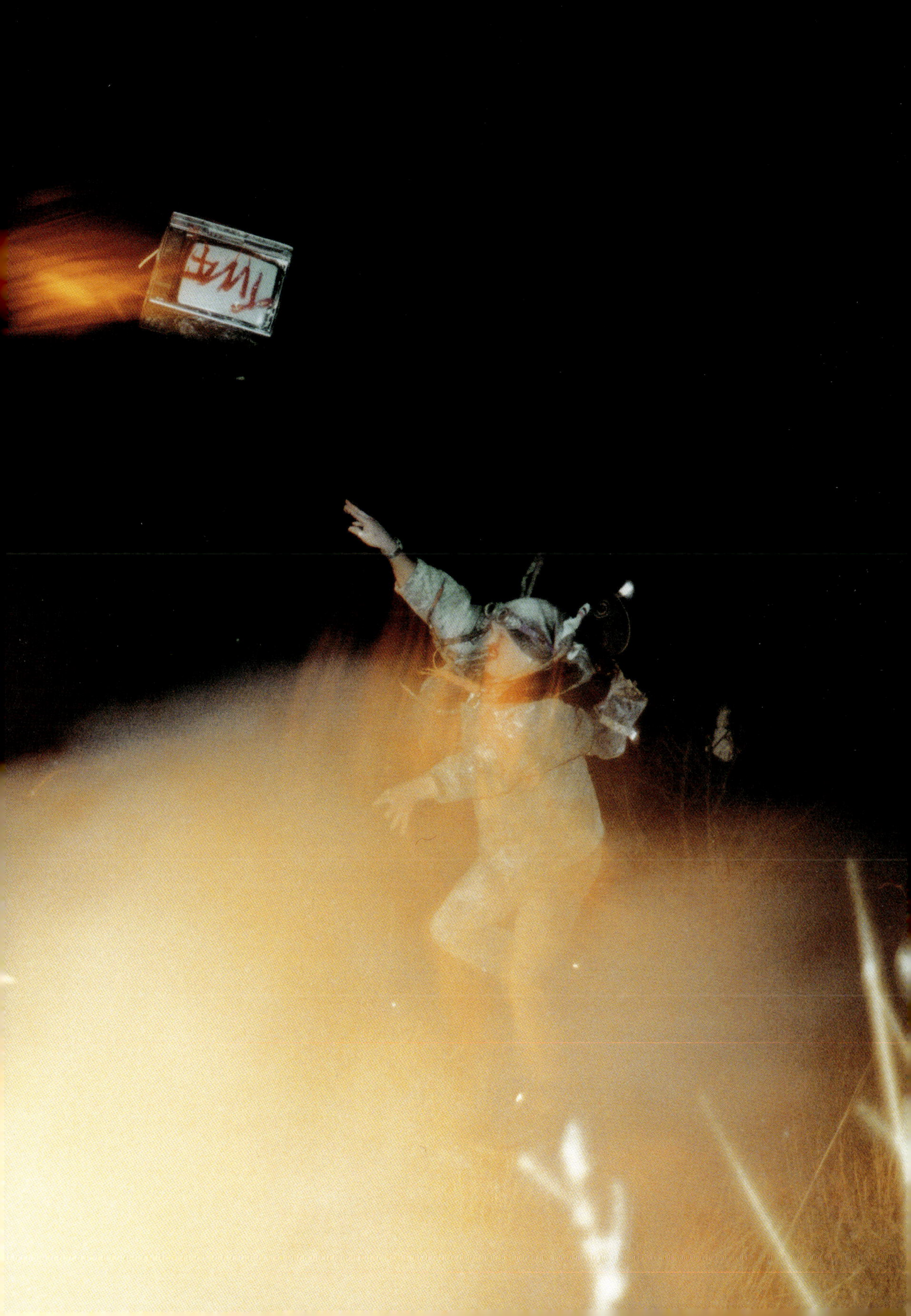

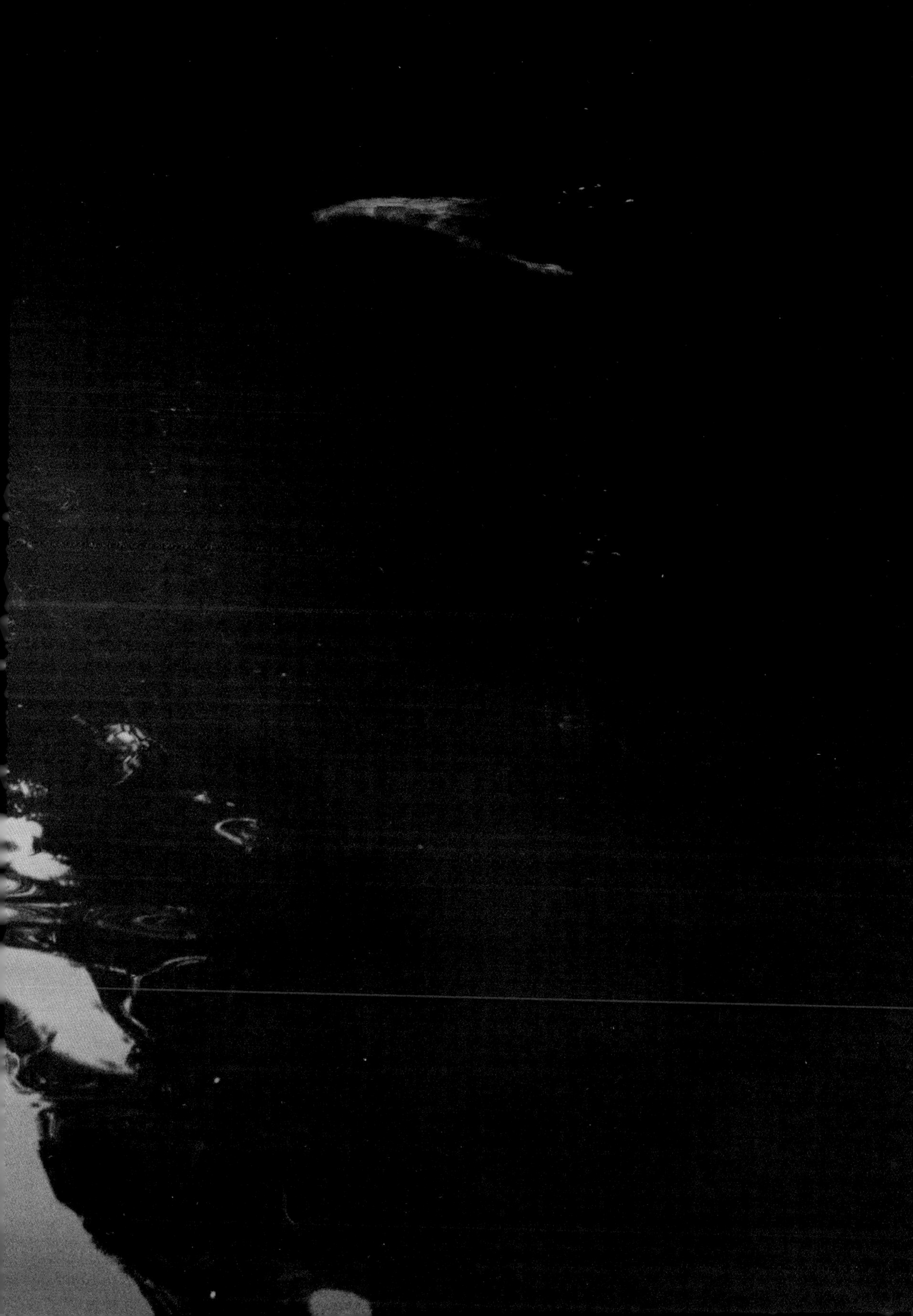

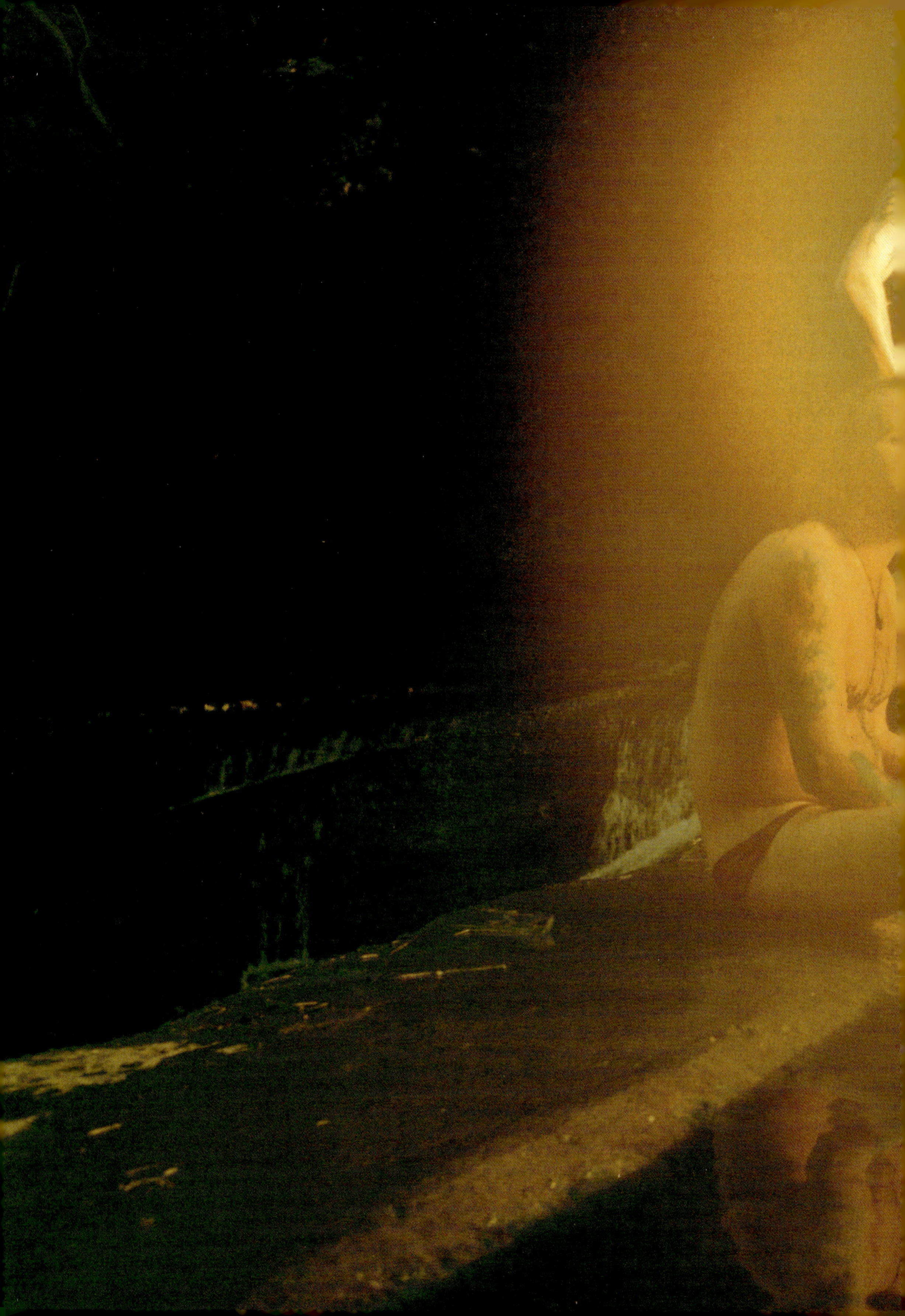

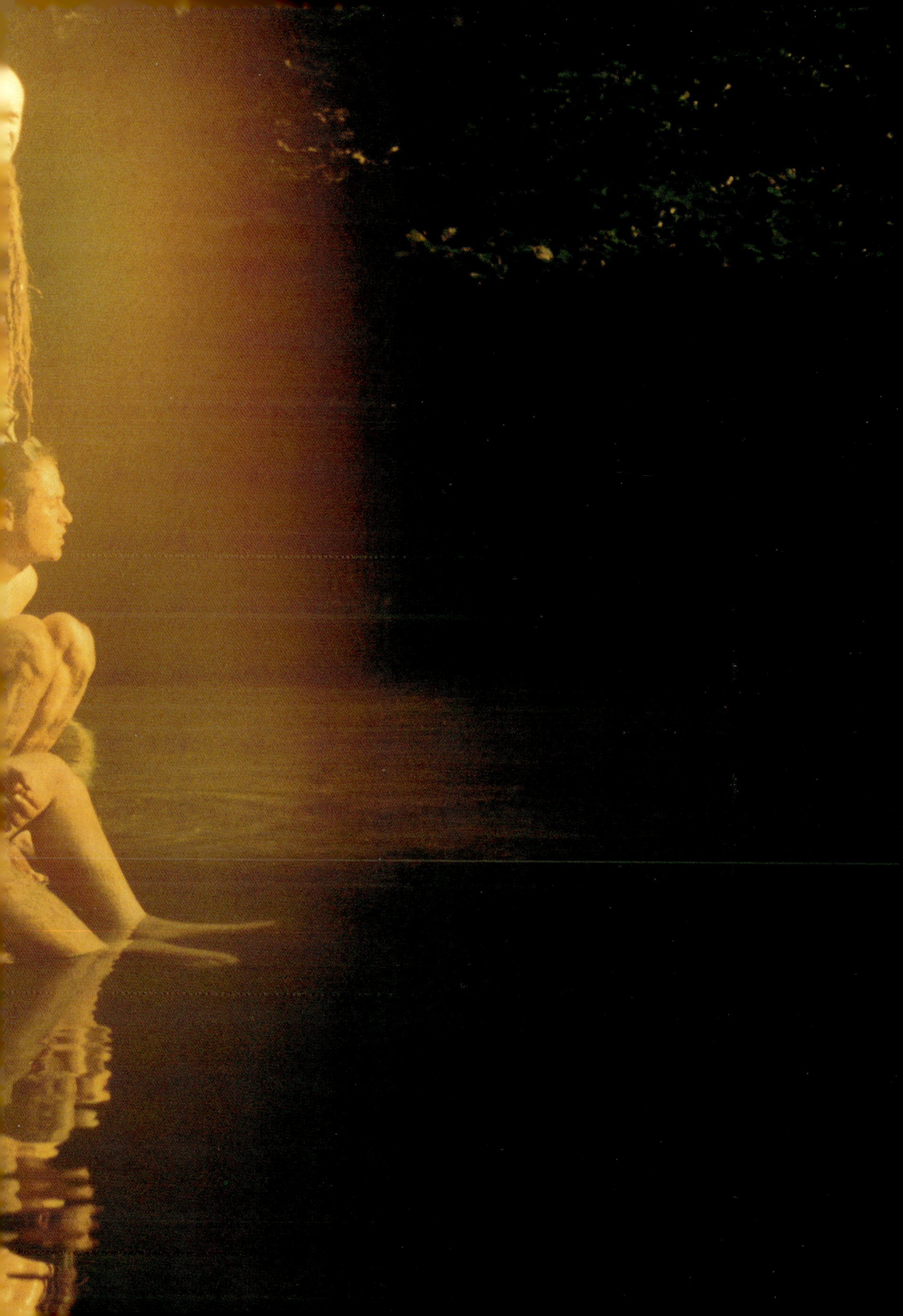

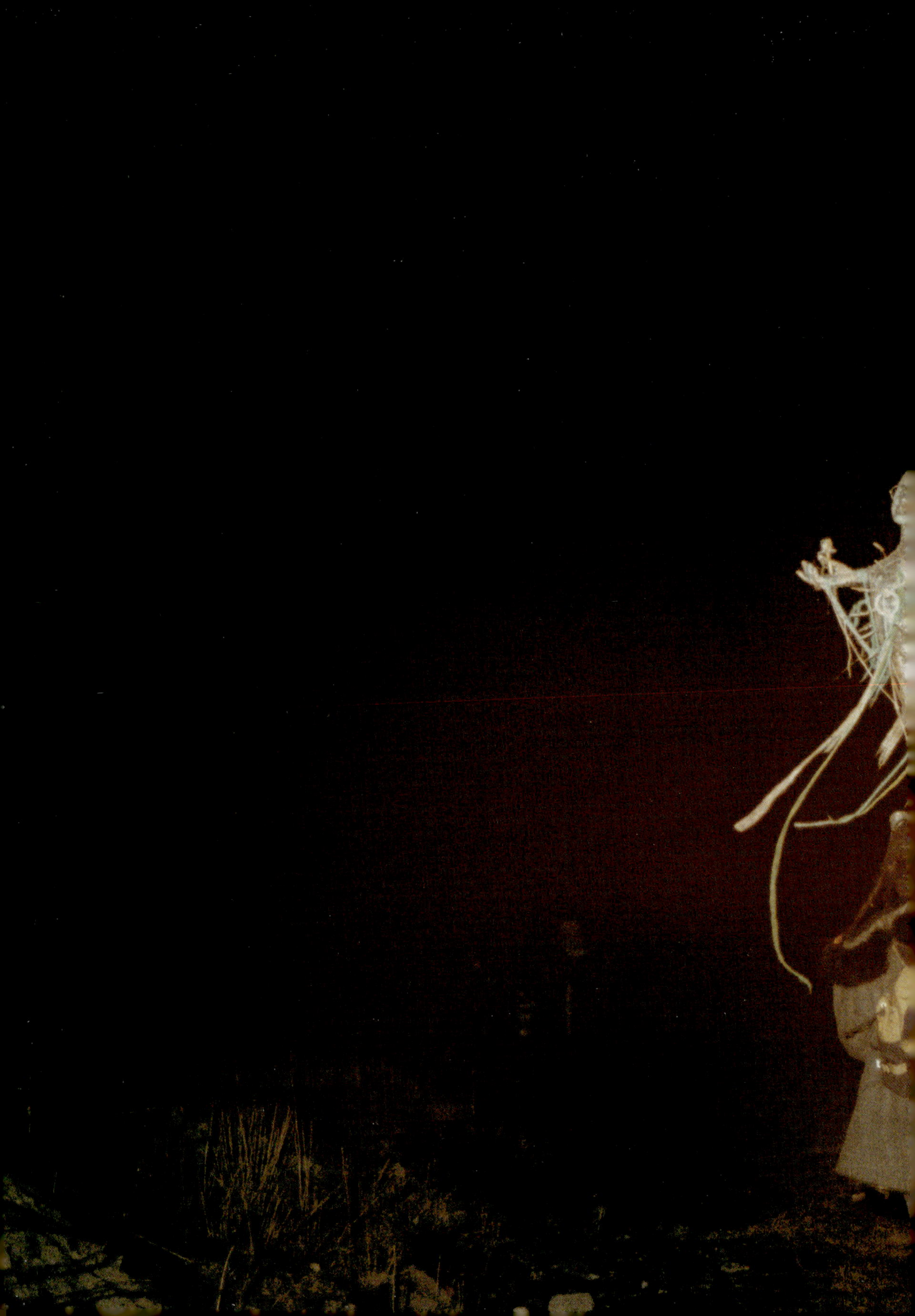